PENGUIN

A FACE IN THE DARK AND OTHER HAUNTINGS

Ruskin Bond's first novel, *The Room on the Roof*, written when he was seventeen, received the John Llewellyn Rhys Memorial Prize in 1957. Since then he has written a number of novellas, essays, poems and children's books, many of which have been published by Penguin. He has also written over 500 short stories and articles that have appeared in magazines and anthologies. He received the Sahitya Akademi Award in 1992, the Padma Shri in 1999 and the Padma Bhushan in 2014.

Ruskin Bond was born in Kasauli, Himachal Pradesh, and grew up in Jamnagar, Dehradun, New Delhi and Shimla. As a young man, he spent four years in the Channel Islands and London. He returned to India in 1955. He now lives in Landour, Mussoorie, with his adopted family.

A FACE IN THE DARK
AND OTHER HAUNTINGS

RUSKIN BOND

PENGUIN BOOKS
An imprint of Penguin Random House

PENGUIN BOOKS

USA | Canada | UK | Ireland | Australia
New Zealand | India | South Africa | China

Penguin Books is part of the Penguin Random House group of companies
whose addresses can be found at global.penguinrandomhouse.com

Published by Penguin Random House India Pvt. Ltd
4th Floor, Capital Tower 1, MG Road,
Gurugram 122 002, Haryana, India

Penguin
Random House
India

First published in Viking by Penguin Books India 2004
Published in Penguin Books 2009

ISBN 9780143067863

Typeset in Sabon Roman by SURYA, New Delhi
Printed at Manipal Technologies Limited, India

www.penguin.co.in

MIX
Paper from
responsible sources
FSC® C043100

CONTENTS

introduction

There are more things in heaven and earth,
                                        Horatio,
Than are dreamt of in your philosophy.

—Shakespeare, *Hamlet*, Act I Scene V

You don't have to believe in ghosts in order to enjoy a ghost story. And while a good ghost story may not turn you into a believer in the supernatural, it can make you ponder upon the mysteries of human existence, and raise the possibility of another layer of life outside our material selves—something of the soul-force, the aura of a person that lingers on after the body is no more. Such a projection of personality may occasionally manifest itself in a visible form, but usually it is an invisible, supernatural phenomenon that makes its presence felt in different, often unexpected ways.

Call it a vision if you will—like the vision I have sometimes had of my father, long dead, looking just as he did when I was a child; or the boy on the storm-swept hillside, there to warn me of impending danger; or the children playing on haunted hill, their images trapped in a fragment of time.

These were helpful, protective apparitions. For ghosts are not intent on frightening us, although the more malevolent among them may do so. (Far more men do evil than ghosts do.) Most visitors from the other side are melancholy spirits looking for a lost love or a lost home. They are unquiet, unhappy souls, haunting the places they once knew. And a house is 'haunted' once it is occupied by one of these restless phantoms from the past. Old houses, in fact, are the most popular places for resident ghosts. Many great writers, from Dickens (*A Christmas Carol*) to Kipling (*The Return of Imray*) to Henry James (*The Turn of the Screw*), have set some of their best-known stories in a haunted house.

In India, the peepal tree takes pride of place in tales of the supernatural. Bhoots, prets, munjias and other unearthly beings all take up residence in this most hospitable tree; and when they get a chance they take possession of unwary passers-by and play havoc with their lives. (I have been warned all my life not to yawn under a peepal tree: 'A mischievous pret will jump down your throat!' And then my life, I am told, will not be my own; even if the pret does not kill me or make me insane, it will completely ruin my digestion.)

The stories in this collection were written at different times during my long writing life. They were written to entertain rather than to instruct. They are not all frightening or spooky, because the supernatural has its funny side too, as some of the stories here will testify.

I have been told that I write about ghosts, jinns, witches and others with empathy, even affection. People find this strange. Perhaps I am a ghost myself, then? Ravi Singh of Penguin India seems to think so. He insists that on one of his visits to Mussoorie, he saw me in the Writers' Bar of the Savoy Hotel at three in the afternoon—a time when I am always in the middle of my afternoon siesta, at the other end of town. Was it a case of personality projection? Did I, in my dreams, feel a great thirst come upon me and travel through time and space in search of refreshment?

'Do you serve spirits?' I apparently asked the bartender. And apparently he complied.

But Ravi doesn't tell me how many he'd had before he saw my 'ghost'.

Mussoorie
June 2004

a face in the dark

Mr Oliver, an Anglo-Indian teacher, was returning to his school late one night, on the outskirts of the hill station of Simla. From before Kipling's time, the school had been run on English public-school lines and the boys, most of them from wealthy Indian families, wore blazers, caps and ties. *Life* magazine, in a feature on India, had once called it the 'Eton of the East'. Mr Oliver had been teaching in the school for several years.

The Simla Bazaar, with its cinemas and restaurants, was about three miles from the school and Mr Oliver, a bachelor, usually strolled into the town in the evening, returning after dark, when he would take a short cut through the pine forest.

When there was a strong wind, the pine trees made sad, eerie sounds that kept most people to the main road. But Mr Oliver was not a nervous or imaginative man. He carried a torch and its gleam—the batteries were running down—moved fitfully down the narrow forest path. When its flickering light fell on the figure of a boy, who was sitting alone on a rock, Mr Oliver stopped. Boys were not supposed to be out after dark.

'What are you doing out here, boy?' asked Mr Oliver sharply, moving closer so that he could recognize the miscreant. But even as he approached the boy, Mr Oliver sensed that something was wrong. The boy appeared to be crying. His head hung down, he held his face in his hands, and his body shook convulsively. It was a strange, soundless weeping and Mr Oliver felt distinctly uneasy.

'Well, what's the matter?' he asked, his anger giving way to concern. 'What are you crying for?' The boy would not answer or look up. His body continued to be racked with silent sobbing. 'Come on, boy, you shouldn't be out here at this hour. Tell me the trouble. Look up!' The boy looked up. He took his hands from his face and looked up at his teacher. The light from Mr Oliver's torch fell

Ruskin Bond

on the boy's face—if you could call it a face.

It had no eyes, ears, nose or mouth. It was just a round smooth head—with a school cap on top of it! And that's where the story should end. But for Mr Oliver it did not end here.

The torch fell from his trembling hand. He turned and scrambled down the path, running blindly through the trees and calling for help. He was still running towards the school buildings when he saw a lantern swinging in the middle of the path. Mr Oliver stumbled up to the watchman, gasping for breath. 'What is it, sahib?' asked the watchman. 'Has there been an accident? Why are you running?'

'I saw something—something horrible—a boy weeping in the forest—and he had no face!'

'No face, sahib?'

'No eyes, nose, mouth—nothing!'

'Do you mean it was like this, sahib?' asked the watchman and raised the lamp to his own face. The watchman had no eyes, no ears, no features at all—not even an eyebrow! And that's when the wind blew the lamp out.

the monkeys

I couldn't be sure, next morning, if I had been dreaming or if I had really heard dogs barking in the night and had seen them scampering about on the hillside below the cottage. There had been a Golden Cocker, a Retriever, a Peke, a Dachshund, a black Labrador, and one or two nondescripts. They had woken me with their barking shortly after midnight, and made so much noise that I got out of bed and looked out of the open window. I saw them quite plainly in the moonlight, five or six dogs rushing excitedly through the long monsoon grass.

It was only because there had been so many breeds among the dogs that I felt a little confused. I had been in the cottage only a week, and I was already on nodding or speaking terms with most of my neighbours. Colonel Fanshawe, retired from the Indian Army, was my immediate neighbour. He did keep a Cocker, but it was black. The elderly Anglo-Indian spinsters who lived beyond the deodars kept only cats. (Though why cats should be the prerogative of spinsters, I have never been able to understand.) The milkman kept a couple of mongrels. And the Punjabi industrialist who had bought a former prince's palace—without ever occupying it—left the property in charge of a watchman who kept a huge Tibetan mastiff.

None of these dogs looked like the ones I had seen in the night.

'Does anyone here keep a Retriever?' I asked Colonel Fanshawe, when I met him taking his evening walk.

'No one that I know of,' he said and gave me a swift, penetrating look from under his bushy eyebrows. 'Why, have you seen one around?'

'No, I just wondered. There are a lot of dogs in the area, aren't there?'

'Oh, yes. Nearly everyone keeps a dog here. Of course every now and then a panther carries one off. Lost a lovely little terrier myself, only last winter.'

Colonel Fanshawe, tall and red-faced,

seemed to be waiting for me to tell him something more—or was he just taking time to recover his breath after a stiff uphill climb?

That night I heard the dogs again. I went to the window and looked out. The moon was at the full, silvering the leaves of the oak trees.

The dogs were looking up into the trees, and barking. But I could see nothing in the trees, not even an owl.

I gave a shout, and the dogs disappeared into the forest.

Colonel Fanshawe looked at me expectantly when I met him the following day. He knew something about those dogs, of that I was certain; but he was waiting to hear what I had to say. I decided to oblige him.

'I saw at least six dogs in the middle of the night,' I said. 'A Cocker, a Retriever, a Peke, a Dachshund, and two mongrels. Now, Colonel, I'm sure you must know whose they are.'

The Colonel was delighted. I could tell by the way his eyes glinted that he was going to enjoy himself at my expense.

'You've been seeing Miss Fairchild's dogs,' he said with smug satisfaction.

'Oh, and where does she live?'

'She doesn't, my boy. Died fifteen years ago.'

Ruskin Bond

'Then what are her dogs doing here?'

'Looking for monkeys,' said the Colonel. And he stood back to watch my reaction.

'I'm afraid I don't understand,' I said.

'Let me put it this way,' said the Colonel. 'Do you believe in ghosts?'

'I've never seen any,' I said.

'But you have, my boy, you have. Miss Fairchild's dogs died years ago—a Cocker, a Retriever, a Dachshund, a Peke, and two mongrels. They were buried on a little knoll under the oaks. Nothing odd about their deaths, mind you. They were all quite old, and didn't survive their mistress very long. Neighbours looked after them until they died.'

'And Miss Fairchild lived in the cottage where I stay? Was she young?'

'She was in her mid-forties, an athletic sort of woman, fond of the outdoors. Didn't care much for men. I thought you knew about her.'

'No, I haven't been here very long, you know. But what was it you said about monkeys? Why were the dogs looking for monkeys?'

'Ah, that's the interesting part of the story. Have you seen the langur monkeys that sometimes come to eat oak leaves?'

'No.'

'You will, sooner or later. There has always

been a band of them roaming these forests. They're quite harmless really, except that they'll ruin a garden if given half a chance . . . Well, Miss Fairchild fairly loathed those monkeys. She was very keen on her dahlias—grew some prize specimens—but the monkeys would come at night, dig up the plants, and eat the dahlia bulbs. Apparently they found the bulbs much to their liking. Miss Fairchild would be furious. People who are passionately fond of gardening often go off balance when their best plants are ruined—that's only human, I suppose. Miss Fairchild set her dogs on the monkeys, whenever she could, even if it was in the middle of the night. But the monkeys simply took to the trees and left the dogs barking.

'Then one day—or rather one night—Miss Fairchild took desperate measures. She borrowed a shotgun, and sat up near a window. And when the monkeys arrived, she shot one of them dead.'

The Colonel paused and looked out over the oak trees which were shimmering in the warm afternoon sun.

'She shouldn't have done that,' he said.

'Never shoot a monkey. It's not only that they're sacred to Hindus—but they are rather human, you know. Well, I must be getting on.

Ruskin Bond

Good day!' And the Colonel, having ended his story rather abruptly, set off at a brisk pace through the deodars.

I didn't hear the dogs that night. But the next day I saw the monkeys—the real ones, not ghosts. There were about twenty of them, young and old, sitting in the trees munching oak leaves. They didn't pay much attention to me, and I watched them for some time.

They were handsome creatures, their fur a silver-grey, their tails long and sinuous. They leapt gracefully from tree to tree, and were very polite and dignified in their behaviour towards each other—unlike the bold, rather crude red monkeys of the plains. Some of the younger ones scampered about on the hillside, playing and wrestling with each other like schoolboys.

There were no dogs to molest them—and no dahlias to tempt them into the garden.

But that night, I heard the dogs again. They were barking more furiously than ever.

'Well, I'm not getting up for them this time,' I mumbled, and pulled the blanket over my ears.

But the barking grew louder, and was joined by other sounds, a squealing and a scuffling.

Then suddenly the piercing shriek of a

woman rang through the forest. It was an unearthly sound, and it made my hair stand up.

I leapt out of bed and dashed to the window.

A woman was lying on the ground, three or four huge monkeys were on top of her, biting her arms and pulling at her throat. The dogs were yelping and trying to drag the monkeys off, but they were being harried from behind by others. The woman gave another blood-curdling shriek, and I dashed back into the room, grabbed hold of a small axe, and ran into the garden.

But everyone—dogs, monkeys and shrieking woman—had disappeared, and I stood alone on the hillside in my pyjamas, clutching an axe and feeling very foolish.

The Colonel greeted me effusively the following day.

'Still seeing those dogs?' he asked in a bantering tone.

'I've seen the monkeys too,' I said.

'Oh, yes, they've come around again. But they're real enough and quite harmless.'

'I know—but I saw them last night with the dogs.'

'Oh, did you really? That's strange, very strange.'

The Colonel tried to avoid my eye, but I hadn't quite finished with him.

'Colonel,' I said. 'You never did get around to telling me how Miss Fairchild died.'

'Oh, didn't I? Must have slipped my memory. I'm getting old, don't remember people as well as I used to. But, of course, I remember about Miss Fairchild, poor lady. The monkeys killed her. Didn't you know? They simply tore her to pieces . . .'

His voice trailed off, and he looked thoughtfully at a caterpillar that was making its way up his walking stick.

'She shouldn't have shot one of them,' he said. 'Never shoot a monkey—they're rather human, you know . . .'

three

the haunted bicycle

I was living at the time in a village about five miles out of Shahganj, a district in east Uttar Pradesh, and my only means of transport was a bicycle. I could of course have gone into Shahganj on any obliging farmer's bullock-cart, but, in spite of bad roads and my own clumsiness as a cyclist, I found the bicycle a trifle faster. I went into Shahganj almost every day, collected my mail, bought a newspaper, drank innumerable cups of tea, and gossiped with the tradesmen. I cycled back to the village at about six in the evening along a quiet, unfrequented forest road. During the winter months it was dark by six, and I would have to use a lamp on the bicycle.

One evening, when I had covered about

half the distance to the village, I was brought to a halt by a small boy who was standing in the middle of the road. The forest at that late hour was no place for a child: wolves and hyenas were common in the district. I got down from my bicycle and approached the boy, but he didn't seem to take much notice of me.

'What are you doing here on your own?' I asked.

'I'm waiting,' he said, without looking at me.

'Waiting for whom? Your parents?'

'No, I am waiting for my sister.'

'Well, I haven't passed her on the road,' I said. 'She may be further ahead. You had better come along with me, we'll soon find her.'

The boy nodded and climbed silently on to the crossbar in front of me. I have never been able to recall his features. Already it was dark and besides, he kept his face turned away from me.

The wind was against us, and as I cycled on, I shivered with the cold, but the boy did not seem to feel it. We had not gone far when the light from my lamp fell on the figure of another child who was standing by the side of the road. This time it was a girl. She was a little older than the boy, and her hair was long and windswept, hiding most of her face.

'Here's your sister,' I said. 'Let's take her along with us.'

The girl did not respond to my smile, and she did no more than nod seriously to the boy. But she climbed up on to my back carrier, and allowed me to pedal off again. Their replies to my friendly questions were monosyllabic, and I gathered that they were wary of strangers. Well, when I got to the village, I would hand them over to the headman, and he could locate their parents.

The road was level, but I felt as though I was cycling uphill. And then I noticed that the boy's head was much closer to my face, that the girl's breathing was loud and heavy, almost as though she was doing the riding. Despite the cold wind, I began to feel hot and suffocated.

'I think we'd better take a rest,' I suggested.

'No!' cried the boy and girl together. 'No rest!'

I was so surprised that I rode on without any argument; and then, just as I was thinking of ignoring their demand and stopping, I noticed that the boy's hands, which were resting on the handlebar, had grown long and black and hairy.

Ruskin Bond

My hands shook and the bicycle wobbled about on the road.

'Be careful!' shouted the children in unison. 'Look where you're going!'

Their tone now was menacing and far from childlike. I took a quick glance over my shoulder and had my worst fears confirmed. The girl's face was huge and bloated. Her legs, black and hairy, were trailing along the ground.

'Stop!' ordered the terrible children. 'Stop near the stream!'

But before I could do anything, my front wheel hit a stone and the bicycle toppled over. As I sprawled in the dust, I felt something hard, like a hoof, hit me on the back of the head, and then there was total darkness.

When I recovered consciousness, I noticed that the moon had risen and was sparkling on the waters of a stream. The children were not to be seen anywhere. I got up from the ground and began to brush the dust from my clothes. And then, hearing the sound of splashing and churning in the stream, I looked up again.

Two small black buffaloes gazed at me from the muddy, moonlit water.

four
___

the vision

It was 1955. I had returned to Dehradun after three years in England, determined to live life on my own terms: India would be my home, and I would be a writer. It was a difficult time. The fifty-pound advance from Andre Deutsch for my first book, *The Room on the Roof*, had melted away, and the book was yet to be published. My mother and stepfather had moved to Delhi with the rest of the family. I did not accompany them because I wanted the freedom to be my very own person. Indeed I had my freedom, and I was young—not yet twenty-one—but the future was uncertain. Sometimes I was lonely and unhappy, and I wondered if I had made the right choices.

I lived in a rented room with a small balcony, but without electricity or running water, above a small provision store in the main bazaar. The landlady had her own battles to fight with life, so she mostly left me alone, but there was the dhobi's son, Sitaram, who had made it his mission to follow me around wherever I went and ruin my peace.

Early one morning I decided I'd take a long cycle ride out of the town's precincts. I'd read all about the dawn coming up like thunder, but had never really got up early enough to witness it. I asked Sitaram to do me a favour and wake me at six. He woke me at five. It was just getting light. As I dressed, the colour of the sky changed from ultramarine to a clear shade of lavender, and then the sun came up gloriously naked.

I had borrowed a cycle from my landlady—it was occasionally used by her servant to deliver purchases to favoured customers—and I rode off down Rajpur Road in a rather wobbly, zig-zag manner, as it was about five years since I had ridden a bicycle. Dehra's traffic is horrific today, but there was not much of it then, and at six in the morning the roads were deserted. In any case, I was soon out of the town and then I reached the tea-gardens. I stopped at a small wayside teashop for refreshment and while I was about to dip a hard bun in my tea, a familiar shadow fell across the table, and I looked up to see Sitaram grinning at me. I'd forgotten—he too had a cycle.

Dear friend and familiar! I did not know whether to be pleased or angry.

'My cycle is faster than yours,' he said.

'Well, then carry on riding it to Rishikesh. I'll try to keep up with you.'

He laughed. 'You can't escape me that way, writer-sahib.'

'Where are you going?' he asked, as I prepared to mount my cycle.

'Anywhere,' I said. 'As far as I feel like going.'

'Come, I will show you roads that you have never seen before.'

Were these prophetic words? Was I to discover new paths and new meanings courtesy of the washerman's son?

'Lead on, light of my life,' I said, and he beamed and set off at a good speed so that I had trouble keeping up with him.

He left the main road, and took a bumpy, dusty path through a bamboo-grove. It was a fairly broad path and we could cycle side by side. It led out of the bamboo grove into an extensive tea-garden, then turned and twisted before petering out beside a small canal.

Ruskin Bond

We rested our cycles against the trunk of a mango tree. The mangoes were beginning to form, but many would be bruised by birds before they could fully ripen.

A flock of parrots circled above us. A kingfisher dived low over the canal and came up with a little gleaming fish.

While Sitaram went exploring the canal banks, I sat down and rested my back against the bole of the mango tree.

Suddenly, a sensation of great peace stole over me. I felt in complete empathy with my surroundings—the gurgle of the canal water, the trees, the birds, the warmth of the sun, the faint breeze, the caterpillar on the grass near my feet, the grass itself, each blade . . .

I began singing an old song of Nelson Eddy's—

> When you are down and out,
> Lift up your head and shout—
> It's going to be a great day!

As I sang, I noticed a movement across the canal. Through some wild babul trees, a dim figure seemed to be approaching. It wasn't Sitaram, it wasn't a stranger, it was someone I knew. Though the figure remained dim, I was soon able to recognize my father's face and form.

He stood there, smiling, and the song died on my lips. I was surrounded by a great, soothing silence.

As I stood up and raised my hand in greeting, the figure faded away.

Perhaps it was the song that had brought my father back for a few seconds. He had always liked Nelson Eddy and collected all his records. Where were they now? Where were the songs of old?

My dear, dear father. How much I had loved him. And I had been only ten when he was snatched away. Now he had given me a sign that he was still with me . . . I wasn't alone. Optimism surged through me.

There was a great splashing close by, and I looked down to see that Sitaram was in the water. I hadn't even noticed him slip off his clothes and jump into the canal.

He beckoned to me to join him, and after a moment's hesitation, I decided to do so, feeling light of mind.

Several days passed, each as unremarkable, if not more, than the day before. Then, coming up the steps to my room one evening, I was struck by the sweet smell of Raat-ki-Rani, Queen of the Night, and I was puzzled by its presence because I knew there was none growing on my balcony or anywhere else in the vicinity. In front of the building stood a neem tree, and a mango tree, the last survivor of the mango grove that had occupied this area before it was cleared away for a shopping block. There were no shrubs around—they would not have survived the traffic or the press of people. Only potted plants occupied the shop-fronts and verandah-spaces. And yet there was that distinct smell of Raat-ki-Rani, growing stronger all the time.

Halfway up the steps, I looked up, and in the half-light of a neighbouring window, I saw my father standing at the top of the steps. He was looking at me the way he had done that day near the canal—with affection and a smile playing on his lips—and at first I stood still, surprised by happiness. Then, waves of love and memories of the old companionship sweeping over me, I advanced up the steps; but when I reached the top, the vision faded and I stood there alone, the sweet smell of Raat-ki-Rani still with me, but no one else, no sound but the distant shunting of an engine.

This was the second time I had seen my father, or rather his apparition. I did not know if it portended anything, or if it was just that he wanted to see me again, and was trying to cross the gulf between our different worlds.

Alone on the balcony, looking down at the badly-lit street, I indulged in a bout of nostalgia, recalling boyhood days when my father was my only companion—in the Royal Air Force tent outside Delhi, with the hot winds of May and June swirling outside during the day and the subtle fragrance of Raat-ki-Rani wafting in at night; for the evening walks in Chotta Shimla, on the road to Bishop Cotton School; and earlier, while exploring the beach at Jamnagar, looking for sea-shells.

I still had one with me—a smooth round shell which must have belonged to a periwinkle. I put it to my ear and heard the hum of the ocean, the siren song of the sea. The sound filled me with a strange restlessness, a longing for a different life. I decided to take a break from the hot and humid town waiting patiently for the monsoon rains.

On the third morning of my voluntary exile from Dehra, I strode up river, taking a well-worn path which led to the shrines in the higher mountains. I was not seeking salvation or enlightenment; I wished merely to come to terms with myself and my situation. Should I

Ruskin Bond

stay on in Dehra, or should I strike out for richer pastures—Delhi or Bombay, perhaps? Or should I return to London and my desk in the Thomas Cook office? Oh, for the life of a clerk! Or I could give English tuitions, I supposed. Except that everyone seemed to know English.

The future looked rather empty as I trudged forlornly up the mountain trail. What I really needed just then was a good companion—someone to confide in, someone with whom to share life's little problems. No wonder people got married! But who would marry an indigent writer with twenty rupees in the bank and no prospects in a land where English was on the way out? (I was not to know that English would be 'in' again, thirty years later.) This depressing thought in mind, I found myself standing on the middle of a small wooden bridge across one of the mountain streams that fed the great river. I wasn't thinking of hurling myself on the rocks below; the thought would have terrified me. Besides, I'm the sort who clings to life no matter how strong the temptation is to leave it. But absent-mindedly I leant against the wooden railing of the bridge. The wood was rotten and gave way immediately.

I fell some thirty feet, fortunately into the middle of the stream where the water was fairly deep. I did not strike any rocks. But the current was swift and carried me along with it. I could swim a little, so I swam and drifted with the current, even though my clothes were an encumbrance. But ahead I saw a greater turbulence and knew I was approaching rapids and, possibly, a waterfall. That would have spelt the end of a promising young writer. So I tried desperately to reach the river bank on my right. I got my hands on a smooth rock but was pulled away by the current. Then I clutched at the branch of a dead tree that had fallen into the stream. I held fast; but I did not have the strength to pull myself out of the water.

A wave of panic rose inside me and it seemed pointless to fight the current any longer. Before I closed my eyes, ready to give up, something made me turn my head a little and look towards the grassy bank to my right. I saw my father standing there. He was smiling at me again, a gentle smile full of love. I needed to reach him. I gripped the branch tightly and made a special effort—yes, I was a stout-hearted boy—heaved myself out of the water and climbed along the waterlogged tree-trunk until I sank into ferns and soft grass.

I looked around, but the vision had gone. The air was scented with wild roses and magnolia.

Looking back on those years, I know that the choices I made then were the right choices for me. And an old, dear companion came back to help me stay the course.

five

————

whistling in the dark

The moon was almost at the full. Bright moonlight flooded the road. But I was stalked by the shadows of the trees, by the crooked oak branches reaching out towards me—some threateningly, others as though they needed companionship.

Once I dreamt that the trees could walk. That on moonlit nights like this they would uproot themselves for a while, visit each other, talk about old times—for they had seen many men and happenings, especially the older ones. And then, before dawn, they would return to the places where they had been condemned to grow. Lonely sentinels of the night. And this was a good night for them to walk. They appeared eager to do so: a restless rustling of leaves, the creaking of branches—these were sounds that came from within them in the silence of the night . . .

Occasionally other strollers passed me in the dark. It was still quite early, just eight o'clock, and some people were on their way home. Others were walking into town for a taste of the bright lights, shops and restaurants. On the unlit road I could not recognize them. They did not notice me. I was reminded of an old song from my childhood. Softly, I began humming the tune, and soon the words came back to me:

> *We three,*
> *We're not a crowd;*
> *We're not even company—*
> *My echo,*
> *My shadow,*
> *And me . . .*

I looked down at my shadow, moving silently beside me. We take our shadows for granted, don't we? There they are, the uncomplaining companions of a lifetime, mute and helpless witnesses to our every act of commission or omission. On this bright moonlit night I could not help noticing you, Shadow, and I was sorry that you had to see so much that I was ashamed of; but glad, too, that you were around when I had my small triumphs. And what of my echo? I thought of calling out to see if my call came back to me; but I refrained from doing so, as I did not wish to disturb the perfect stillness of the mountains or the conversations of the trees.

The road wound up the hill and levelled out at the top, where it became a ribbon of moonlight entwined between tall deodars. A flying squirrel glided across the road, leaving one tree for another. A nightjar called. The rest was silence.

The old cemetery loomed up before me. There were many old graves—some large and monumental—and there were a few recent graves too, for the cemetery was still in use. I could see flowers scattered on one of them—a few late dahlias and scarlet salvia. Further on, near the boundary wall, part of the cemetery's retaining wall had collapsed in the heavy monsoon rains. Some of the tombstones had come down with the wall. One grave lay exposed. A rotting coffin and a few scattered bones were the only relics of someone who had lived and loved like you and me.

Part of the tombstone lay beside the road, but the lettering had worn away. I am not

Ruskin Bond

normally a morbid person, but something made me stoop and pick up a smooth round shard of bone, probably part of a skull. When my hand closed over it, the bone crumbled into fragments. I let them fall to the grass. Dust to dust.

And from somewhere, not too far away, came the sound of someone whistling.

At first I thought it was another late-evening stroller, whistling to himself much as I had been humming my old song. But the whistler approached quite rapidly; the whistling was loud and cheerful. A boy on a bicycle sped past. I had only a glimpse of him, before his cycle went weaving through the shadows on the road.

But he was back again in a few minutes. And this time he stopped a few feet away from me, and gave me a quizzical half-smile. A slim dusky boy of fourteen or fifteen. He wore a school blazer and a yellow scarf. His eyes were pools of liquid moonlight.

'You don't have a bell on your cycle,' I said.

He said nothing, just smiled at me with his head a little to one side. I put out my hand, and I thought he was going to take it. But then, quite suddenly, he was off again, whistling cheerfully though rather tunelessly. A whistling schoolboy. A bit late for him to be out, but he seemed an independent sort.

The whistling grew fainter, then faded away altogether. A deep sound-denying silence fell upon the forest. My shadow and I walked home.

Next morning I woke to a different kind of whistling—the song of the thrush outside my window.

It was a wonderful day, the sunshine warm and sensuous, and I longed to be out in the open. But there was work to be done, proofs to be corrected, letters to be written. And it was several days before I could walk to the top of the hill, to that lonely tranquil resting place under the deodars. It seemed to me ironic that those who had the best view of the glistening snow-capped peaks were all buried several feet underground.

Some repair work was going on. The retaining wall of the cemetery was being shored up, but the overseer told me that there was no money to restore the damaged grave. With the help of the chowkidar, I returned the scattered bones to a little hollow under the collapsed masonry, and I left some money with him so that he could have the open grave bricked up.

The name on the gravestone had worn away, but I could make out a date—20 November 1950—some fifty years ago, but not too long ago as gravestones go . . .

I found the burial register in the church vestry and turned back the yellowing pages to 1950, when I was just a schoolboy myself. I found the name there—Michael Dutta, aged fifteen—and the cause of death: road accident.

Well, I could only make guesses. And to turn conjecture into certainty, I would have to find an old resident who might remember the boy or the accident.

There was old Miss Marley at Pine Top. A retired teacher from Woodstock, she had a wonderful memory, and she had lived in the hill station for more than half a century.

White-haired and smooth-cheeked, her bright blue eyes full of curiosity, she gazed benignly at me through her old-fashioned pince-nez.

'Michael was a charming boy—full of exuberance, always ready to oblige. I had only to mention that I needed a newspaper or an Aspirin, and he'd be off on his bicycle, swooping down these steep roads with great abandon. But these hills roads, with their sudden corners, weren't meant for racing around on a bicycle.

They were widening our road for motor traffic, and a truck was coming uphill, loaded with rubble, when Michael came round a bend and smashed headlong into it. He was rushed to the hospital, and the doctors did their best, but he did not recover consciousness. Of course you must have seen his grave. That's why you're here. His parents? They left shortly afterwards. Went abroad, I think . . . A charming boy, Michael, but just a bit too reckless. You'd have liked him, I think.'

I did not see the phantom bicycle-rider again for some time, although I felt his presence on more than one occasion. And when on a cold winter's evening, I walked past that lonely cemetery, I thought I heard him whistling far away. But he did not manifest himself. Perhaps it was only the echo of a whistle, in communion with my insubstantial shadow.

It was several months before I saw that smiling face again. And then it came at me out of the mist as I was walking home in drenching monsoon rain. I had been to a dinner party at the old community centre, and I was returning home along a very narrow, precipitous path known as the Eyebrow. A storm had been threatening all evening. A heavy mist had settled on the hillside. It was so thick that the light from my torch simply bounced off it. The sky blossomed with sheet lightning and thunder rolled over the mountains. The rain became heavier. I moved forward slowly, carefully, hugging the hillside. There was a clap of thunder, and then I saw him emerge from the mist and stand in my way—the same slim dark youth who had materialized near the cemetery. He did not smile. Instead he put up his hand and waved me back. I hesitated, stood still. The mist lifted a little, and I saw that the path had disappeared. There was a gaping emptiness a few feet in front of me. And then a drop of over a hundred feet to the rocks below.

As I stepped back, clinging to a thorn bush for support, the boy vanished. I stumbled back to the community centre and spent the night on a chair in the library.

I did not see him again.

But weeks later, when I was down with a severe bout of flu, I heard him from my sickbed, whistling beneath my window. Was he calling to me to join him, I wondered, or was he just trying to reassure me that all was well? I got out of bed and looked out, but I saw no one. From time to time I heard his whistling; but as

I got better, it grew fainter until it ceased altogether.

Fully recovered, I renewed my old walks to the top of the hill. But although I lingered near the cemetery until it grew dark, and paced up and down the deserted road, I did not see or hear the whistler again. I felt lonely, in need of a friend, even if it was only a phantom bicycle-rider. But there were only the trees.

And so every evening I walk home in the darkness, singing the old refrain:

> *We three,*
> *We're not alone,*
> *We're not even company—*
> *My echo,*
> *My shadow,*
> *And me . . .*

reunion at the regal

If you want to see a ghost, just stand outside New Delhi's Regal Cinema for twenty minutes or so. The approach to the grand old cinema hall is a great place for them. Sooner or later you'll see a familiar face in the crowd. Before you have time to recall who it was or who it may be, it will have disappeared and you will be left wondering if it really was so-and-so . . . because surely so-and-so died several years ago . . .

The Regal was very posh in the early 1940s when, in the company of my father, I saw my first film there. The Connaught Place cinemas still had a new look about them, and they showed the latest offerings from Hollywood and Britain. To see a Hindi film, you had to travel all the way to Kashmere Gate or Chandni Chowk.

Over the years, I was in and out of the Regal quite a few times, and so I became used to meeting old acquaintances or glimpsing familiar faces in the foyer or on the steps outside.

On one occasion, I was mistaken for a ghost.

I was about thirty at the time. I was standing on the steps of the arcade, waiting for someone, when a young Indian man came up to me and said something in German or what sounded like German.

'I'm sorry,' I said. 'I don't understand. You may speak to me in English or Hindi.'

'Aren't you Hans? We met in Frankfurt last year.'

'I'm sorry, I've never been to Frankfurt.'

'You look exactly like Hans.'

'Maybe I'm his double. Or maybe I'm his ghost!'

My facetious remark did not amuse the young man. He looked confused and stepped back, a look of horror spreading over his face. 'No, no,' he stammered. 'Hans is alive, you can't be his ghost!'

'I was only joking.'

Ruskin Bond

But he had turned away, hurrying off through the crowd. He seemed agitated. I shrugged philosophically. So I had a double called Hans, I reflected, perhaps I'd run into him some day.

I mention this incident only to show that most of us have look-alikes, and that sometimes we see what we *want* to see, or are looking for, even if on looking closer, the resemblance isn't all that striking.

But there was no mistaking Kishen when he approached me. I hadn't seen him for five or six years, but he looked much the same. Bushy eyebrows, offset by gentle eyes; a determined chin, offset by a charming smile. The girls had always liked him, and he knew it; and he was content to let them do the pursuing.

We saw a film—I think it was *The Wind Cannot Read*—and then we strolled across to the old Standard Restaurant, ordered dinner and talked about old times, while the small band played sentimental tunes from the 1950s.

Yes, we talked about old times—growing up in Simla, where we lived next door to each other, exploring our neighbours' lichee orchards, cycling about the town in the days before the scooter had been invented, kicking a football around on the maidan, or just sitting on the compound wall doing nothing. I had just finished school, and an entire year stretched before me until it was time to go abroad. Kishen's father, a civil engineer, was under transfer orders, so Kishen too temporarily did not have to go to school.

He was an easy-going boy, quite content to be at a loose end in my company. I had literary pretensions; he was apparently without ambition although, as he grew older, he was to surprise me by his wide reading and erudition.

One day, while we were cycling along the bank of the Raipur canal, he skidded off the path and fell into the canal with his cycle. The water was only waist-deep; but it was quite swift, and I had to jump in to help him. There was no real danger, but we had some difficulty getting the cycle out of the canal.

Later, he learnt to swim.

But that was after I'd gone away . . .

Convinced that my prospects would be better in England, my mother packed me off to her relatives in Jersey, and it was to be four long years before I could return to the land I truly cared for. In that time, many of my Simla friends had left the town; it wasn't a place where you could do much after finishing school.

Kishen wrote to me from Calcutta, where he was at an engineering college. Then he was off to 'study abroad'. I heard from him from time to time. He seemed happy. He had an equable temperament and got on quite well with most people. He had a girlfriend too, he told me.

'But,' he wrote, 'you're my oldest and best friend. Wherever I go, I'll always come back to see you.'

And of course he did. We met several times while I was living in Delhi, and once we revisited Simla together and walked down Rajpur Road and ate tikkees and golguppas behind the clock tower. But the old familiar faces were missing. The streets were overbuilt and overcrowded, and the lichee gardens were fast disappearing. After we got back to Delhi, Kishen accepted the offer of a job in Bombay. We kept in touch in desultory fashion, but our paths and our lives had taken different directions. He was busy nurturing his career with an engineering firm; I had retreated to the hills with radically different goals—to write and be free of the burden of a ten-to-five desk job.

Time went by, and I lost track of Kishen. Some years later, I was standing in the lobby of the India International Centre, when an attractive young woman in her mid-thirties came up to me and said, 'Hello, Rusty, don't you remember me? I'm Manju. I lived next to you and Kishen and Ranbir when we were children.'

I recognized her then, for she had always been a pretty girl, the 'belle' of Simla's Mall Road.

We sat down and talked about old times and new times, and I told her that I hadn't heard from Kishen for a few years.

'Didn't you know?' she asked. 'He died about two years ago.'

'What happened?' I was dismayed, even angry, that I hadn't heard about it. 'He couldn't have been more than thirty-eight.'

'It was an accident on a beach in Goa. A child had got into difficulties and Kishen swam out to save her. He did rescue the little girl, but when he swam ashore he had a heart attack. He died right there on the beach. It seems he had always had a weak heart. The exertion must have been too much for him.'

I was silent. I knew he'd become a fairly good swimmer, but I did not know about the heart.

'Was he married?' I asked.

Ruskin Bond

'No, he was always the eligible bachelor boy.'

It had been good to see Manju again, even though she had given me bad news. She told me she was happily married, with a small son. We promised to keep in touch.

And that's the end of this tale, apart from my brief visit to Delhi the next year.

I had taken a taxi to Connaught Place and decided to get down at the Regal. I stood there a while, undecided about what to do or where to go. It was almost time for a show to start, and there were a lot of people milling around.

I thought someone called my name. I looked around, and there was Kishen in the crowd.

'Kishen!' I called, and started after him.

But a stout lady climbing out of a scooter rickshaw got in my way, and by the time I had a clear view again, my old friend had disappeared.

Had I seen his look-alike, a double? Or had he kept his promise to come back to see me once more?

wilson's bridge

The old wooden bridge has gone, and today an iron suspension bridge straddles the Bhagirathi as it rushes down the gorge below Gangotri. But villagers will tell you that you can still hear the hoofs of Wilson's horse as he gallops across the bridge he had built a hundred and fifty years ago. At the time people were sceptical of its safety, and so to prove its sturdiness, he rode across it again and again. Parts of the old bridge can still be seen on the far bank of the river. And the legend of Wilson and his pretty hill bride, Gulabi, is still well-known in this region.

I had joined some friends in the old forest rest house near the river. There were the Rays, recently married, and the Dattas, married many years. The younger Rays quarrelled frequently; the older Dattas looked on with more amusement than concern. I was a part of their group and yet something of an outsider. As a single man, I was a person of no importance. And as a marriage counsellor, I wouldn't have been of any use to them.

I spent most of my time wandering along the river banks or exploring the thick deodar and oak forests that covered the slopes. It was these trees that had made a fortune for Wilson and his patron, the Raja of Tehri. They had exploited the great forests to the full, floating huge logs downstream to the timber yards in the plains.

Returning to the rest house late one evening, I was halfway across the bridge when I saw a figure at the other end, emerging from the mist. Presently I made out a woman, wearing the plain dhoti of the hills; her hair fell loose over her shoulders. She appeared not to see me, and reclined against the railing of the bridge, looking down at the rushing waters far below. And then, to my amazement and horror, she climbed over the railing and threw herself into the river.

I ran forward, calling out, but I reached the railing only to see her fall into the foaming waters below, where she was carried swiftly downstream.

The watchman's cabin stood a little way off. The door was open. The watchman, Ram Singh, was reclining on his bed, smoking a hookah.

'Someone just jumped off the bridge,' I said breathlessly. 'She's been swept down the river!'

The watchman was unperturbed. 'Gulabi again,' he said, almost to himself; and then to me, 'Did you see her clearly?'

'Yes, a woman with long loose hair—but I didn't see her face very clearly.'

'It must have been Gulabi. Only a ghost, my dear sir. Nothing to be alarmed about. Every now and then someone sees her throw herself into the river. Sit down,' he said, gesturing towards a battered old armchair, 'be comfortable and I'll tell you all about it.'

I was far from comfortable, but I listened to Ram Singh tell me the tale of Gulabi's suicide. After making me a glass of hot sweet tea, he launched into a long rambling account of how Wilson, a British adventurer seeking his fortune, had been hunting musk deer when he encountered Gulabi on the path from her village. The girl's grey-green eyes and peach-blossom complexion enchanted him, and he went out of his way to get to know her people. Was he in love with her or did he simply find her beautiful

Ruskin Bond

and desirable? We shall never really know. In the course of his travels and adventures he had known many women, but Gulabi was different, childlike and ingenuous, and he decided he would marry her. The humble family to which she belonged had no objection. Hunting had its limitations, and Wilson found it more profitable to trap the region's great forest wealth. In a few years he had made a fortune. He built a large timbered house at Harsil, another in Dehradun, and a third at Mussoorie. Gulabi had all she could have wanted, including two robust little sons. When he was away on work, she looked after their children and their large apple orchard at Harsil.

And then came the evil day when Wilson met the Englishwoman, Ruth, on the Mussoorie mall, and decided that she should have a share of his affections and his wealth. A fine house was provided for her too. The time he spent at Harsil with Gulabi and his children dwindled. 'Business affairs'—he was now one of the owners of a bank—kept him in the fashionable hill resort. He was a popular host and took his friends and associates on shikar parties in the Doon.

Gulabi brought up her children in village style. She heard stories of Wilson's dalliance with the Mussoorie woman and, on one of his rare visits, she confronted him and voiced her resentment, demanding that he leave the other woman. He brushed her aside and told her not to listen to idle gossip. When he turned away from her, she picked up the flintlock pistol that lay on the gun table, and fired one shot at him. The bullet missed him and shattered her looking-glass. Gulabi ran out of the house, through the orchard and into the forest, then down the steep path to the bridge built by Wilson only two or three years before. When he had recovered his composure, he mounted his horse and came looking for her. It was too late. She had already thrown herself off the bridge into the swirling waters far below. Her body was found a mile or two downstream, caught between some rocks.

This was the tale that Ram Singh told me, with various flourishes and interpolations of his own. I thought it would make a good story to tell my friends that evening, before the fireside in the rest house. They found the story fascinating, but when I told them I had seen Gulabi's ghost, they thought I was doing a little embroidering of my own. Mrs Dutta thought it was a tragic tale. Young Mrs Ray thought Gulabi had been very silly. 'She was a simple girl,' opined Mr Dutta. 'She responded in the only way she knew . . .' 'Money can't buy happiness,' said Mr Ray. 'No,' said Mrs Dutta, 'but it can buy you a great many comforts.' Mrs Ray wanted to talk of other things, so I changed the subject. It can get a little confusing for a bachelor who must spend the evening with two married couples. There are undercurrents which he is aware of but not equipped to deal with.

I would walk across the bridge quite often after that. It was busy with traffic during the day, but after dusk there were only a few vehicles on the road and seldom any pedestrians. A mist rose from the gorge below and obscured the far end of the bridge. I preferred walking there in the evening, half-expecting, half-hoping to see Gulabi's ghost again. It was her face that I really wanted to see. Would she still be as beautiful as she was fabled to be?

It was on the evening before our departure that something happened that would haunt me for a long time afterwards.

There was a feeling of restiveness as our days there drew to a close. The Rays had apparently made up their differences, although they weren't talking very much. Mr Dutta was anxious to get back to his office in Delhi and

Mrs Dutta's rheumatism was playing up. I was restless too, wanting to return to my writing desk in Mussoorie.

That evening I decided to take one last stroll across the bridge to enjoy the cool breeze of a summer's night in the mountains. The moon hadn't come up, and it was really quite dark, although there were lamps at either end of the bridge providing sufficient light for those who wished to cross over.

I was standing in the middle of the bridge, in the darkest part, listening to the river thundering down the gorge, when I saw the sari-draped figure emerging from the lamplight and making towards the railings.

Instinctively I called out, 'Gulabi!'

She half-turned towards me, but I could not see her clearly. The wind had blown her hair across her face and all I saw was wildly staring eyes. She raised herself over the railing and threw herself off the bridge. I heard the splash as her body struck the water far below.

Once again I found myself running towards the part of the railing where she had jumped. And then someone was running towards the same spot, from the direction of the rest house. It was young Mr Ray.

'My wife!' he cried out. 'Did you see my wife?'

Ruskin Bond

He rushed to the railing and stared down at the swirling waters of the river.

'Look! There she is!' He pointed at a helpless figure bobbing about in the water.

We ran down the steep bank to the river but the current had swept her on. Scrambling over rocks and bushes, we made frantic efforts to catch up with the drowning woman. But the river in that defile is a roaring torrent, and it was over an hour before we were able to retrieve poor Mrs Ray's body, caught in driftwood about a mile downstream.

She was cremated not far from where we found her and we returned to our various homes in gloom and grief, chastened but none the wiser for the experience.

If you happen to be in that area and decide to cross the bridge late in the evening, you might see Gulabi's ghost or hear the hoofbeats of Wilson's horse as he canters across the old wooden bridge looking for her. Or you might see the ghost of Mrs Ray and hear her husband's anguished cry. Or there might be others. Who knows?

eight

topaz

It seemed strange to be listening to the strains of *The Blue Danube* while gazing out at the pine-clad slopes of the Himalayas, worlds apart. And yet the music of the waltz seemed singularly appropriate. A light breeze hummed through the pines, and the branches seemed to move in time to the music. The record player was new, but the records were old, picked up in a junk shop behind the Mall.

Below the pines there were oaks, and one oak tree in particular caught my eye. It was the biggest of the lot and stood by itself on a little knoll below the cottage. The breeze was not strong enough to lift its heavy old branches, but something was moving, swinging gently from the tree, keeping time to the music of the waltz, dancing . . .

It was someone hanging from the tree.

A rope oscillated in the breeze, the body turned slowly, turned this way and that, and I saw the face of a girl, her hair hanging loose, her eyes sightless, hands and feet limp; just turning, turning, while the waltz played on.

I turned off the player and ran downstairs.

Down the path through the trees, and on to the grassy knoll where the big oak stood.

A long-tailed magpie took fright and flew out from the branches, swooping low across the ravine. In the tree there was no one, nothing. A great branch extended halfway across the knoll, and it was possible for me to reach up and touch it. A girl could not have reached it without climbing the tree.

As I stood there, gazing up into the branches, someone spoke behind me.

'What are you looking at?'

I swung round. A girl stood in the clearing, facing me, a girl of seventeen or eighteen; alive, healthy, with bright eyes and a tantalizing smile. She was lovely to look at. I hadn't seen such a pretty girl in years.

'You startled me,' I said. 'You came up so unexpectedly.'

'Did you see anything—in the tree?' she asked.

'I thought I saw someone from my window. That's why I came down. Did *you* see anything?'

'No.' She shook her head, the smile leaving her face for a moment. 'I don't see anything. But other people do—sometimes.'

'What do they see?'

'My sister.'

'Your *sister*?'

'Yes. She hanged herself from this tree. It was many years ago. But sometimes you can see her hanging there.'

She spoke matter-of-factly: whatever had happened seemed very remote to her.

We both moved some distance away from the tree. Above the knoll, on a disused private tennis court (a relic from the hill station's colonial past) was a small stone bench. She sat down on it, and, after a moment's hesitation, I sat down beside her.

'Do you live close by?' I asked.

'Further up the hill. My father has a small bakery.'

She told me her name—Hameeda. She had two younger brothers.

'You must have been quite small when your sister died.'

'Yes. But I remember her. She was pretty.'

'Like you.'

She laughed in disbelief. 'Oh, I am nothing compared to her. You should have seen my sister.'

'Why did she kill herself?'

'Because she did not want to live. That's the only reason, no? She was to have been married but she loved someone else, someone who was not of her own community. It's an old story and the end is always sad, isn't it?'

'Not always. But what happened to the boy—the one she loved? Did he kill himself too?'

'No, he took a job in some other place. Jobs are not easy to get, are they?'

'I don't know. I've never tried for one.'

'Then what do you do?'

'I write stories.'

'Do people *buy* stories?'

'Why not? If your father can sell bread, I can sell stories.'

'People must have bread. They can live without stories.'

'No, Hameeda, you're wrong. People can't live without stories.'

Hameeda! I couldn't help loving her. Just loving her. No fierce desire or passion had taken hold of me. It wasn't like that. I was happy just to look at her, watch her while she sat on the grass outside my cottage, her lips stained with the juice of wild bilberries. She chatted away—about her friends, her clothes, her favourite things.

'Won't your parents mind if you come here every day?' I asked.

'I have told them you are teaching me.'

'Teaching you what?'

'They did not ask. You can tell me stories.'

So I told her stories.

It was midsummer.

The sun glinted on the ring she wore on her third finger: a translucent golden topaz, set in silver.

'That's a pretty ring,' I remarked.

'You wear it,' she said, impulsively removing it from her hand. 'It will give you good thoughts. It will help you to write better stories.'

She slipped it on to my little finger.

'I'll wear it for a few days,' I said. 'Then you must let me give it back to you.'

On a day that promised rain I took the path down to the stream at the bottom of the hill. There I found Hameeda gathering ferns from the shady places along the rocky ledges above the water.

'What will you do with them?' I asked.

'This is a special kind of fern. You can cook it as a vegetable.'

'It is tasty?'

'No, but it is good for rheumatism.'

'Do you suffer from rheumatism?'

'Of course not. They are for my grandmother, she is very old.'

'There are more ferns further upstream,' I said. 'But we'll have to get into the water.'

We removed our shoes and began paddling upstream. The ravine became shadier and narrower, until the sun was almost completely shut out. The ferns grew right down to the water's edge. We bent to pick them but instead found ourselves in each other's arms; and sank slowly, as in a dream, into the soft bed of ferns, while overhead a whistling thrush burst out in dark sweet song.

'It isn't time that's passing by,' it seemed to say. 'It is you and I. It is you and I . . .'

I waited for her the following day, but she did not come.

Several days passed without my seeing her.

Was she sick? Had she been kept at home? Had she been sent away? I did not even know where she lived, so I could not ask. And if I had been able to ask, what would I have said?

Then one day I saw a boy delivering bread and pastries at the little tea shop about a mile down the road. From the upward slant of his eyes, I caught a slight resemblance to Hameeda. As he left the shop, I followed him up the hill. When I came abreast of him, I asked: 'Do you have your own bakery?'

He nodded cheerfully, 'Yes. Do you want anything—bread, biscuits, cakes? I can bring them to your house.'

'Of course. But don't you have a sister? A girl called Hameeda?'

His expression changed. He was no longer friendly. He looked puzzled and slightly apprehensive.

'Why do you want to know?'

'I haven't seen her for some time.'

'We have not seen her either.'

'Do you mean she has gone away?'

'Didn't you know? You must have been away a long time. It is many years since she died. She killed herself. You did not hear about it?'

'But wasn't that her sister—your other sister?'

'I had only one sister—Hameeda—and she died, when I was very young. It's an old story, ask someone else about it.'

He turned away and quickened his pace, and I was left standing in the middle of the road, my head full of questions that couldn't be answered.

That night there was a thunderstorm. My bedroom window kept banging in the wind. I got up to close it and, as I looked out, there was a flash of lightning and I saw that frail body again, swinging from the oak tree.

I tried to make out the features, but the head hung down and the hair was blowing in the wind.

Was it all a dream?

It was impossible to say. But the topaz on my hand glowed softly in the darkness. And a whisper from the forest seemed to say, 'It isn't time that's passing by, my friend. It is you and I . . .'

the black cat

Before the cat came, of course there had to be a broomstick.

In the bazaar of one of our hill stations is an old junk shop—dirty, dingy and dark—in which I often potter about looking for old books or Victorian bric-a-brac. Sometimes one comes across useful household items, but I do not usually notice these. I was, however, attracted to an old but well-preserved broom standing in a corner of the shop. A long-handled broom was just what I needed. I had no servant to sweep out the rooms of my cottage, and I did not enjoy bending over double when using the common short-handled *jharoo*.

The old broom was priced at ten rupees. I haggled with the shopkeeper and got it for five.

It was a strong broom, full of character, and I used it to good effect almost every morning. And there this story might have ended—or would never have begun—if I had not found the large black cat sitting on the garden wall.

The black cat had bright yellow eyes, and it gave me a long penetrating look, as though it were summing up my possibilities as an exploitable human. Though it miaowed once or twice, I paid no attention. I did not care much for cats. But when I went indoors, I found that the cat had followed and begun scratching at the pantry door.

It must be hungry, I thought, and gave it some milk.

The cat lapped up the milk, purring deeply all the while, then sprang up on a cupboard and made itself comfortable.

Well, for several days there was no getting rid of that cat. It seemed completely at home, and merely tolerated my presence in the house. It was more interested in my broom than me, and would dance and skittle around the broom whenever I was sweeping the rooms. And when the broom was resting against the wall, the cat would sidle up to it, rubbing itself against the handle and purring loudly.

A cat and a broomstick—the combination was suggestive, full of possibilities . . . The cottage was old, almost a hundred years old, and I wondered about the kind of tenants it might have had during these long years. I had been in the cottage only for a year. And though it stood alone in the midst of a forest of Himalayan oaks, I had never encountered any ghosts or spirits.

Miss Bellows came to see me in the middle of July. I heard the tapping of a walking stick on the rocky path outside the cottage, a tapping which stopped near the gate.

'Mr Bond!' called an imperious voice. 'Are you at home?'

I had been doing some gardening, and looked up to find an elderly straight-backed Englishwoman peering at me over the gate.

'Good evening,' I said, dropping my hoe.

'I believe you have my cat,' said Miss Bellows.

Though I had not met the lady before, I knew her by name and reputation. She was the oldest resident in the hill station.

'I do have a cat,' I said, 'though it's probably more correct to say that the cat has me. If it's your cat, you're welcome to it. Why don't you come in while I look for her?'

Miss Bellows stepped in. She wore a rather old-fashioned black dress, and her ancient but strong walnut stick had two or three curves in it and a knob instead of a handle.

She made herself comfortable in an armchair while I went in search of the cat. But the cat was on one of her mysterious absences, and though I called for her in my most persuasive manner, she did not respond. I knew she was probably quite near. But cats are like that—perverse obstinate creatures.

When finally I returned to the sitting room, there was the cat, curled up on Miss Bellows' lap.

'Well, you've got her, I see. Would you like some tea before you go?'

'No, thank you,' said Miss Bellows. 'I don't drink tea.'

'Something stronger, perhaps. A little brandy?' She looked up at me rather sharply. Disconcerted, I hastened to add, 'Not that I drink much, you know. I keep a little in the house for emergencies. It helps ward off colds and things. It's particularly good for—er—well, for colds,' I finished lamely.

'I see your kettle's boiling,' she said. 'Can I have some hot water?'

'Hot water? Certainly.' I was a little puzzled,

but I did not want to antagonize Miss Bellows at our first meeting.

'Thank you. And a glass.'

She took the glass and I went to get the kettle. From the pocket of her voluminous dress, she extracted two small packets, similar to those containing chemists' powders. Opening both packets, she poured first a purple powder and then a crimson powder into the glass. Nothing happened.

'Now the water, please,' she said.

'It's boiling hot!'

'Never mind.'

I poured boiling water into her glass, and there was a terrific fizzing and bubbling as the frothy stuff rose to the rim. It gave off a horrible stench. The potion was so hot that I thought it would crack the glass; but before this could happen, Miss Bellows put it to her lips and drained the contents.

'I think I'll be going now,' she said, putting the glass down and smacking her lips. The cat, tail in the air, voiced its agreement. Said Miss Bellows, 'I'm much obliged to you, young man.'

'Don't mention it,' I said humbly. 'Always at your service.'

She gave me her thin bony hand, and held mine in an icy grip.

Ruskin Bond

I saw Miss Bellows and the black cat to the gate, and returned pensively to my sitting room. Living alone was beginning to tell on my nerves and imagination. I made a half-hearted attempt to laugh at my fancies, but the laugh stuck in my throat. I couldn't help noticing that the broom was missing from its corner.

I dashed out of the cottage and looked up and down the path. There was no one to be seen. In the gathering darkness I could hear Miss Bellows' laughter, followed by a snatch of song:

> With the darkness round me growing,
> And the moon behind my hat,
> You will soon have trouble knowing
> Which is witch and witch's cat.

Something whirred overhead like a Diwali rocket.

I looked up and saw them silhouetted against the rising moon. Miss Bellows and her cat were riding away on my broomstick.

whispering in the dark

A wild night. Wind moaning, trees lashing themselves in a frenzy, rain beating down on the road, thunder over the mountains. Loneliness stretched ahead of me, a loneliness of the heart as well as a physical loneliness. The world was blotted out by a mist that had come up from the valley, a thick, white, clammy shroud.

I groped through the forest, groped in my mind for the memory of a mountain path, some remembered rock or ancient deodar. Then a streak of blue lightning gave me a glimpse of a barren hillside and a house cradled in mist.

It was an old-world house, built of limestone rock on the outskirts of a crumbling hill station. There was no light in its windows; probably the electricity had been disconnected long ago. But if I could get in it would do for the night.

I had no torch, but at times the moon shone through the wild clouds, and trees loomed out of the mist like primeval giants. I reached the front door and found it locked from within. I walked round to the side and broke a window-pane, put my hand through shattered glass and found the bolt.

The window, warped by over a hundred monsoons, resisted at first. Then it yielded, and I climbed into the mustiness of a long-closed room, and the wind came in with me, scattering papers across the floor and knocking some unidentifiable object off a table. I closed the window, bolted it again; but the mist crawled through the broken glass, and the wind rattled in it like a pair of castanets.

There were matches in my pocket. I struck three before a light flared up.

I was in a large room, crowded with furniture. Pictures on the walls. Vases on the mantelpiece. A candlestand. And, strangely enough, no cobwebs. For all its external look of neglect and dilapidation, the house had been cared for by someone. But before I could notice anything else, the match burnt out.

As I stepped further into the room, the old

deodar flooring creaked beneath my weight. By the light of another match I reached the mantelpiece and lit the candle, noticing at the same time that the candlestick was a genuine antique with cutglass hangings. A deserted cottage with good furniture and glass. I wondered why no one had ever broken in. And then realized that I had just done so.

I held the candlestick high and glanced round the room. The walls were hung with several water-colours and portraits in oils. There was no dust anywhere. But no one answered my call, no one responded to my hesitant knocking. It was as though the occupants of the house were in hiding, watching me obliquely from dark corners and chimneys.

I entered a bedroom and found myself facing a full-length mirror. My reflection stared back at me as though I were a stranger, as though my reflection belonged to the house, while I was only an outsider.

As I turned from the mirror, I thought I saw someone, something, some reflection other than mine, move behind me in the mirror. I caught a glimpse of whiteness, a pale oval face, burning eyes, long tresses, golden in the candlelight. But when I looked in the mirror again there was nothing to be seen but my own pallid face.

Ruskin Bond

A pool of water was forming at my feet. I set the candle down on a small table, found the edge of the bed—a large old four-poster—sat down, and removed my soggy shoes and socks. Then I took off my clothes and hung them over the back of a chair.

I stood naked in the darkness, shivering a little. There was no one to see me—and yet I felt oddly exposed, almost as though I had stripped in a room full of curious people.

I got under the bedclothes—they smelt slightly of eucalyptus and lavender—but found there was no pillow. That was odd. A perfectly made bed, but no pillow! I was too tired to hunt for one. So I blew out the candle—and the darkness closed in around me, and the whispering began . . .

The whispering began as soon as I closed my eyes. I couldn't tell where it came from. It was all around me, mingling with the sound of the wind coughing in the chimney, the stretching of old furniture, the weeping of trees outside in the rain.

Sometimes I could hear what was being said. The words came from a distance: a distance not so much of space as of time . . .

'Mine, mine, he is all mine . . .'

'He is ours, dear, ours.'

Whispers, echoes, words hovering around me with bats' wings, saying the most inconsequential things with a logical urgency. 'You're late for supper . . .'

'He lost his way in the mist.'

'Do you think he has any money?'

'To kill a turtle you must first tie its legs to two posts.'

'We could tie him to the bed and pour boiling water down his throat.'

'No, it's simpler this way.'

I sat up. Most of the whispering had been distant, impersonal, but this last remark had sounded horribly near.

I relit the candle and the voices stopped. I got up and prowled around the room, vainly looking for some explanation for the voices. Once again I found myself facing the mirror, staring at my own reflection and the reflection of that other person, the girl with the golden hair and shining eyes. And this time she held a pillow in her hands. She was standing behind me.

I remembered then the stories I had heard as a boy, of two spinster sisters—one beautiful, one plain—who lured rich, elderly gentlemen into their boarding-house and suffocated them in the night. The deaths had appeared quite natural, and they had got away with it for years. It was only the surviving sister's death-bed confession that had revealed the truth—and even then no one had believed her.

But that had been many, many years ago, and the house had long since fallen down . . .

When I turned from the mirror, there was no one behind me. I looked again, and the reflection had gone.

I crawled back into the bed and put the candle out. And I slept and dreamt (or was I awake and did it really happen?) that the woman I had seen in the mirror stood beside the bed, leant over me, looked at me with eyes flecked by orange flames. I saw people moving in those eyes. I saw myself. And then her lips touched mine, lips so cold, so dry, that a shudder ran through my body.

And then, while her face became faceless and only the eyes remained, something else continued to press down upon me, something soft, heavy and shapeless, enclosing me in a suffocating embrace. I could not turn my head or open my mouth. I could not breathe.

I raised my hands and clutched feebly at the thing on top of me. And to my surprise it came away. It was only a pillow that had somehow fallen over my face, half suffocating me while I dreamt of a phantom kiss.

I flung the pillow aside. I flung the bedclothes from me. I had had enough of whispering, of ownerless reflections, of pillows that fell on me in the dark. I would brave the storm outside rather than continue to seek rest in this tortured house.

I dressed quickly. The candle had almost guttered out. The house and everything in it belonged to the darkness of another time; I belonged to the light of day.

I was ready to leave. I avoided the tall mirror with its grotesque rococo design. Holding the candlestick before me, I moved cautiously into the front room. The pictures on the walls sprang to life.

One, in particular, held my attention, and I moved closer to examine it more carefully by the light of the dwindling candle. Was it just my imagination, or was the girl in the portrait the woman of my dream, the beautiful pale reflection in the mirror? Had I gone back in tiine, or had time caught up with me?

I turned to leave, and the candle gave one final sputter and went out, plunging the room in darkness. I stood still for a moment, trying to collect my thoughts, to still the panic that came rushing upon me. Just then there was a knocking on the door.

Ruskin Bond

'Who's there?' I called.

Silence. And then, again, the knocking, and this time a voice, low and insistent: 'Please let me in, please let me in . . .'

I stepped forward, unbolted the door, and flung it open.

She stood outside in the rain. Not the pale, beautiful one, but a wizened old hag with bloodless lips and flaring nostrils and—but where were the eyes? No eyes, no eyes!

She swept past me on the wind, and at the same time I took advantage of the open doorway to run outside, to run gratefully into the pouring rain, to be lost for hours among the dripping trees, to be glad for all the leeches clinging to my flesh.

And when, with the dawn, I found my way at last, I rejoiced in birdsong and the sunlight piercing and scattering the clouds.

And today if you were to ask me if the old house is still there or not, I would not be able to tell you, for the simple reason that I haven't the slightest desire to go looking for it.

the wind on
haunted hill

Who—whoo—whooo, cried the wind as it swept down from the Himalayan snows. It hurried over the hills and passes, and hummed and moaned in the tall pines and deodars.

On Haunted Hill there was little to stop the wind—only a few stunted trees and bushes, and the ruins of what had once been a small settlement.

On the slopes of the next hill there was a small village. People kept large stones on their tin roofs to prevent them from blowing away. There was nearly always a wind in these parts. Even on sunny days, doors and windows rattled, chimneys choked, clothes blew away.

Three children stood beside a low stone

wall, spreading clothes out to dry. On each garment they placed a rock. Even then the clothes fluttered like flags and pennants.

Usha, dark-haired, rose-cheeked, struggled with her grandfather's long loose shirt. She was eleven or twelve. Her younger brother, Suresh, was doing his best to hold down a bedsheet while Binya, a slightly older girl, Usha's friend and neighbour, was handing them the clothes, one at a time.

Once they were sure everything was on the wall, firmly held down by rocks, they climbed up on the flat stones and sat there for a while, in the wind and the sun, staring across the fields at the ruins on Haunted Hill.

'I must go to the bazaar today,' said Usha.

'I wish I could come too,' said Binya. 'But I have to help with the cows and the housework. Mother isn't well.'

'I can come!' said Suresh. He was always ready to visit the bazaar, which was three miles away on the other side of Haunted Hill.

'No, you can't,' said Usha. 'You must help Grandfather chop wood.'

Their father was in the army, posted in a distant part of the country, and Suresh and his grandfather were the only men in the house. Suresh was eight, chubby and almond-eyed.

'Won't you be afraid to come back alone?' he asked.

'Why should I be afraid?'

'There are ghosts on the hill.'

'I know, but I will be back before it gets dark. Ghosts don't appear during the day.'

'Are there many ghosts in the ruins?' asked Binya.

'Grandfather says so. He says that many years ago—over a hundred years ago—English people lived on the hill. But it was a bad spot, always getting struck by lightning, and they had to move to the next range and build another place.'

'But if they went away, why should there be any ghosts?'

'Because—Grandfather says—during a terrible storm one of the houses was hit by lightning and everyone in it was killed. Everyone, including the children.'

'Were there many children?'

'There were two of them. A brother and sister. Grandfather says he has seen them many times, when he has passed through the ruins late at night. He has seen them playing in the moonlight.'

'Wasn't he frightened?'

'No. Old people don't mind seeing ghosts.'

Usha set out on her walk to the bazaar at two in the afternoon. It was about an hour's walk. She went through the fields, now turning yellow with flowering mustard, then along the saddle of the hill, and up to the ruins.

The path went straight through the ruins. Usha knew it well; she had often taken it while going to the bazaar to do the weekly shopping, or to see her aunt who lived in the town.

Wild flowers grew in the crumbling walls. A wild plum tree grew straight out of the floor of what had once been a large hall. Its soft white blossoms had begun to fall. Lizards scuttled over the stones, while a whistling-thrush, its deep purple plumage glistening in the soft sunshine, sat in an empty window and sang its heart out.

Usha sang to herself, as she tripped lightly along the path. Soon she had left the ruins behind. The path dipped steeply down to the valley and the little town with its straggling bazaar.

Usha took her time in the bazaar. She bought soap and matches, spices and sugar (none of these things could be had in the village, where there was no shop), and a new pipestem for her grandfather's hookah, and an exercise book for Suresh to do his sums in. As an afterthought, she bought him some marbles. Then she went to a *mochi*'s shop to have her mother's slippers repaired. The *mochi* was busy, so she left the slippers with him and said she'd be back in half an hour.

She had two rupees of her own saved up, and she used the money to buy herself a necklace of amber-coloured beads from the old Tibetan lady who sold charms and trinkets from a tiny shop at the end of the bazaar.

There she met her Aunt Lakshmi, who took her home for tea.

Usha spent an hour in Aunt Lakshmi's little flat above the shops, listening to her aunt talk about the ache in her left shoulder and the stiffness in her joints. She drank two cups of sweet hot tea, and when she looked out of the window she saw that dark clouds had gathered over the mountains.

Usha ran to the cobbler's and collected her mother's slippers. The shopping bag was full. She slung it over her shoulder and set out for the village.

Strangely, the wind had dropped. The trees were still, not a leaf moved. The crickets were silent in the grass. The crows flew round in circles, then settled down for the night in an oak tree.

'I must get home before dark,' said Usha to herself, as she hurried along the path. But already the sky was darkening. The clouds, black and threatening, loomed over Haunted Hill. This was March, the month for storms.

A deep rumble echoed over the hills, and Usha felt the first heavy drop of rain hit her cheek.

She had no umbrella with her; the weather had seemed so fine just a few hours ago. Now all she could do was tie an old scarf over her head, and pull her shawl tight across her shoulders. Holding the shopping bag close to her body, she quickened her pace. She was almost running. But the raindrops were coming down faster now. Big, heavy pellets of rain.

A sudden flash of lightning lit up the hill. The ruins stood out in clear outline. Then all was dark again. Night had fallen.

'I won't get home before the storm breaks,' thought Usha. 'I'll have to shelter in the ruins.' She could only see a few feet ahead, but she knew the path well and she began to run.

Suddenly, the wind sprang up again and brought the rain with a rush against her face. It was cold, stinging rain. She could hardly keep her eyes open.

The wind grew in force. It hummed and

whistled. Usha did not have to fight against it. It was behind her now, and helped her along, up the steep path and on to the brow of the hill.

There was another flash of lightning, followed by a peal of thunder. The ruins loomed up before her, grim and forbidding.

She knew there was a corner where a piece of old roof remained. It would give some shelter. It would be better than trying to go on. In the dark, in the howling wind, she had only to stray off the path to go over a rocky cliff edge.

Who—whoo—whooo, howled the wind. She saw the wild plum tree swaying, bent double, its foliage thrashing against the ground. The broken walls did little to stop the wind.

Usha found her way into the ruined building, helped by her memory of the place and the constant flicker of lightning. She began moving along the wall, hoping to reach the sheltered corner. She placed her hands flat against the stones and moved sideways. Her hand touched something soft and furry. She gave a startled cry and took her hand away. Her cry was answered by another cry—half snarl, half screech—and something leapt away in the darkness.

It was only a wild cat. Usha realized this when she heard it. The cat lived in the ruins, and she had often seen it. But for a moment she had been very frightened. Now, she moved quickly along the wall until she heard the rain drumming on the remnant of the tin roof.

Once under it, crouching in the corner, she found some shelter from the wind and the rain. Above her, the tin sheets groaned and clattered, as if they would sail away at any moment. But they were held down by the solid branch of a straggling old oak tree.

Usha remembered that across this empty room stood an old fireplace and that there might be some shelter under the blocked-up chimney. Perhaps it would be drier than it was in her corner; but she would not attempt to find it just now. She might lose her way altogether.

Her clothes were soaked and the water streamed down from her long black hair to form a puddle at her feet. She stamped her feet to keep them warm. She thought she heard a faint cry—was it the cat again, or an owl?—but the sound of the storm blotted out all other sounds.

There had been no time to think of ghosts, but now that she was there, without any plans for venturing out again, she remembered Grandfather's story about the lightning-blasted ruins. She hoped and prayed that lightning would not strike *her* as she sheltered there.

Thunder boomed over the hills, and the lightning came quicker now, only a few seconds between each burst of lightning.

Then there was a bigger flash than most, and for a second or two the entire ruin was lit up. A streak of blue sizzled along the floor of the building, in at one end and out at the other. Usha was staring straight ahead. As the opposite wall was lit up, she saw, crouching in the disused fireplace, two small figures—they could only have been children!

The ghostly figures looked up, staring back at Usha. And then everything was dark again.

Usha's heart was in her mouth. She had seen, without a shadow of a doubt, two ghostly creatures at the other side of the room, and she wasn't going to remain in that ruined building a minute longer.

She ran out of her corner, ran towards the big gap in the wall through which she had entered. She was halfway across the open space when something—someone—fell against her. She stumbled, got up and again bumped into something. She gave a frightened scream.

Someone else screamed. And then there was a shout, a boy's shout, and Usha instantly recognized the voice.

'Suresh!'

'Usha!'

'Binya!'

'It's me!'

'It's us!'

They fell into each other's arms, so surprised and relieved that all they could do was laugh and giggle and repeat each other's names.

Then Usha said, 'I thought you were ghosts.'

'We thought *you* were a ghost!' said Suresh.

'Come back under the roof,' said Usha.

They huddled together in the corner chattering excitedly.

'When it grew dark, we came looking for you,' said Binya. 'And then the storm broke.'

'Shall we run back together?' asked Usha. 'I don't want to stay here any longer.'

'We'll have to wait,' said Binya. 'The path has fallen away at one place. It won't be safe in the dark, in all this rain.'

'Then we may have to wait till morning,' said Suresh. 'And I'm feeling hungry!'

The wind and rain continued, and so did the thunder and lightning, but they were not afraid now. They gave each other warmth and confidence. Even the ruins did not seem so forbidding.

After an hour the rain stopped, and although the wind continued to blow, it was now taking the clouds away, so that the thunder grew more distant. Then the wind too, moved on, and all was silent.

Towards dawn the whistling-thrush began to sing. Its sweet broken notes flooded the rainwashed ruins with music.

'Let's go,' said Usha.

'Come on,' said Suresh. 'I'm hungry.'

As it grew lighter, they saw that the plum tree stood upright again, although it had lost all its blossoms.

They stood outside the ruins, on the brow of the hill, watching the sky grow pink. A light breeze had sprung up.

When they were some distance from the ruins, Usha looked back and said, 'Can you see something there, behind the wall? It's like a hand waving.'

'I can't see anything,' said Suresh.

'It's just the top of the plum tree,' said Binya.

They were on the path leading across the saddle of the hill.

'Goodbye, goodbye . . .'

Voices on the wind.

'Who said goodbye?' asked Usha.

'Not I,' said Suresh.

'Not I,' said Binya.

'I heard someone calling.'

'It's only the wind.'

Usha looked back at the ruins. The sun had come up and was touching the top of the walls. The leaves of the plum tree shone. The thrush sat there, singing.

'Come on,' said Suresh. '*I'm hungry.*'

'Goodbye, goodbye, goodbye, goodbye . . .'

Usha heard them calling. Or was it just the wind?

twelve

the ghost in the garden

Behind the house there was an orchard where guava, lichee and papaya trees mingled with two or three tall mango trees. The guava trees were easy to climb. The lichee trees gave a lot of shade—as well as bunches of delicious lichees in the summer. The mango trees were at their most attractive in the spring, when their blossoms gave out a heady fragrance.

But there was one old mango tree, near the boundary wall, where no one, not even Dhuki the gardener, ever went.

'It doesn't give any fruit,' said Dhuki, when I questioned him. 'It's an old tree.'

'Then why don't we cut it down?'

'We will, one day, when your grandmother wishes . . .'

The weeds grew thick in that corner of the garden. They were safe there from Dhuki's relentless weeding.

'Why doesn't anyone go to that corner of the orchard?' I asked Miss Kellner, our crippled tenant, who had been in Dehra since she was a girl.

But she didn't want to talk about it. Uncle Ken, too, changed the subject whenever I brought it up.

So I wandered about the orchard on my own, cautiously making my way towards that neglected and forbidden corner of the garden until Dhuki called me back.

'Don't go there, *baba*,' he cautioned. 'It's unlucky.'

'Why doesn't anyone go near the old mango tree?' I asked Granny.

She just shook her head and turned away. There was obviously something that no one wanted me to know. So I disobeyed and ignored everyone, and in the still of the afternoon, when most of the household was taking a siesta, I walked over to the old mango tree at the end of the garden.

It was a cool, shady place, and seemed friendly enough. But there were no birds in the tree; no squirrels, either. And this was unusual.

I sat down on the grass, with my back against the trunk of the tree, and peered out at the sunlit house and garden. In the shimmering heat haze I thought I saw someone walking through the trees, but it wasn't Dhuki or anyone I knew.

It had been a hot day, but presently I began to feel cold; and then I found myself shivering, as though a fever had suddenly come on. I looked up into the tree, and the branch above me was moving, swaying slightly, although there was no breeze and all the other leaves and branches were still.

I felt I had to get out of the cold, but I found it difficult to get up. So I crawled across the grass on my hands and knees, until I was in the bright sunlight. The shivering passed and I ran across to the house and did not look back at the mango tree until I had reached the veranda.

I told Miss Kellner about my experience.

'Were you frightened?' she asked.

'Yes—a little,' I confessed.

'And did you see anything?'

'Some of the branches moved—I felt very cold—but there was no wind.'

'Did you hear anything?'

'Just a soft moaning sound.'

Ruskin Bond

'It's an old tree. It groans when it feels its age—just as I do!'

I did not go near the mango tree for some time, and I did not mention the incident to Granny or Uncle Ken. I had by now realized that the subject was taboo with them.

As a boy I was always exploring lonely places—neglected gardens and orchards, unoccupied houses, patches of scrub or wasteland, the fields outside the town, the fringes of the forest. On one of my rambles behind the bungalow, I pushed my way through a thicket of lantana bushes and stumbled over a thick stone slab, twisting my ankle slightly as I fell. For some time I sat on the grass massaging my foot. When the pain eased, I looked more closely at the stone slab and was surprised to find that it was a gravestone. It was almost entirely covered by ivy; obviously no one had been near it for years. I tugged at the ivy and some of it came away in my hands. There was some indistinct lettering on the grave, half-obscured by grass and moss. I could make out a name—Rose—but little more.

I sat there for some time, pondering over my discovery, and wondering why 'Rose' should have been buried at so lonely a spot when there was a cemetery not far away. Why hadn't she been interred beside her kith and kind? Had she wished it so? And why?

Only Miss Kellner seemed willing to answer my questions, and it was to her I went, where she sat in her armchair under the pomalo tree—the armchair from which she never moved except when she was carried bodily to her bed or bathroom by the ayah or a couple of her rickshaw boys. I can never forget crippled Miss Kellner in her armchair in the garden, playing patience with a well-worn pack of cards—and always patient with me whenever I interrupted her game with endless questions about neighbours or relatives or her own history. Even as a boy, the past fascinated me. I don't mean the history of nations; I mean individual histories, the way people lived, and why they were happy or unhappy, and why they sometimes did terrible things for no apparent rhyme or reason.

'Miss Kellner,' I asked, 'whose grave is that in the jungle behind the house?'

She looked at me over the rim of her pince-nez. 'How would you expect me to know, child? Do I look as though I could climb walls, looking for old graves? Have you asked your grandmother?'

Ruskin Bond

'Granny won't tell me anything. And Uncle Ken pretends to know everything when he knows nothing.'

'So how should I know?'

'You've been here a long time.'

'Only twenty years. That happened before I came to this house.'

'*What* happened?'

'Oh, you are a trying boy. Why must you know everything?'

'It's better than *not* knowing.'

'Are you sure? Sometimes it's better not to know.'

'Sometimes, maybe . . . But I *like* to know. Who was Rose?'

'Your grandfather's first wife.'

'Oh.' This came as a surprise. I hadn't heard about grandfather's first marriage. 'But why is she buried in such a lonely place? Why not in the cemetery?'

'Because she took her own life. And in those days a suicide couldn't be given Christian burial in a cemetery. Now is your curiosity satisfied?'

But my appetite had only been whetted for more information. 'And why did she commit suicide?'

'I really don't know, child. Why would

anyone? Because they are unhappy, tired of living, in distress over something or the other.'

'You're not tired of living, are you? Even though you can't walk and your fingers are all crooked . . .'

'Don't be rude, or you won't find any meringues in my pantry! My fingers are good enough for writing, and for poking small boys in the ribs.' And she gave me a sharp poke which made me yelp. 'No, I'm not tired of life—not yet—but people are made differently, you know. And your grandfather isn't around to tell us what happened. And of course he married again—your grandmother . . .'

'Would *she* have known the first one?'

'I don't think so. She met your grandfather much later. But she doesn't like to talk about these things.'

'And how did Rose commit suicide?'

'I have no idea.'

'Of course you know, Miss Kellner. You can't bluff me. You know everything!'

'I wasn't here, I tell you.'

'But you heard all about it. And *I* know how she did it. She must have hanged herself from that mango tree—the tree at the end of the garden, which everyone avoids. I told you I went there one day, and it was very cold and lonely in its shade. I was frightened, you know.'

'Yes,' said Miss Kellner pensively. 'She must have been lonely, poor thing. She wasn't very stable, I'm told. Used to wander about on her own, picking wildflowers, singing to herself, sometimes getting lost and coming home at odd hours. How does the old song go? *Lonely as the desert breeze* . . . In her croaky voice, Miss Kellner sang a refrain from an old ballad, before continuing, 'Your grandfather was very fond of her. He wasn't a cruel man. He put up with her strange ways. But sometimes he lost patience and scolded her and once or twice had even to lock her up. *That* was frightening, because then she would start screaming. It was a mistake locking her up. Never lock anyone up, child . . . Something seemed to snap inside her. She became violent at times.'

'How do you know all this, Miss Kellner?'

'Your grandfather would sometimes come over and tell me his troubles. I was living in another house then, a little way down the road. Poor man, he had a trying time with Rose. He was thinking of sending her to Ranchi, to the mental hospital. Then, early one morning, he found her hanging from the mango tree. Her spirit had flown away, like the bluebird she always wanted to be.'

After that, I did not go near the old mango tree; I found it rather menacing, as though it had actually participated in that dark deed. Poor innocent tree, being saddled with the emotions of unbalanced humans! But I did visit the neglected grave and cleaned the weeds away, so that the inscription came out more clearly: 'Rose, dearly beloved wife of Henry—' (my maternal grandfather's surname followed). And when Dhuki wasn't looking, I plucked a red rose from the garden and placed it on the grave.

One afternoon, when Granny was at a bridge-party and Uncle Ken was taking a walk, I rummaged through the storeroom adjoining the back veranda, leafing through old scrapbooks and magazines. Behind a pile of books I discovered an old wind-up gramophone, an album of well-preserved gramophone records, and a box of steel needles. I took the gramophone into the sitting-room and tried out one of the records. It sounded all right. So I played a few more. They were all songs of yesteryear, romantic ballads sung by tenors and baritones who were popular in the 1920s and '30s. Granny did not listen to music, and the gramophone had been neglected a long time. Now, for the first time in many years, the room was full of melody. *One Alone, I'll See You Again, Will You Remember?, Only A Rose* . . .

> *Only a rose*
> *to give you,*
> *Only a song*
> *dying away,*
> *Only a smile*
> *to keep in memory*

It was while this tender love song was playing that a transformation seemed to come over the room.

At first it grew darker. Then a soft pink glow suffused the room, and I saw the figure of a woman, a smiling melancholy woman in white, drifting, rather than walking, towards me. She stopped in the centre of the room, and appeared to be watching me. She wore the long flowing dress of an earlier day, and her hair was arranged in a sort of coiffure that I'd seen in old photographs.

As the song came to an end, the apparition vanished. The room was normal again. I put away the gramophone and the records. I felt disturbed rather than afraid, and I did not wish to conjure up further emanations from the past.

But in my dreams that night I saw the beautiful sad lady again. She was waltzing in the garden, sometimes by herself, sometimes partnered by other phantom dancers. She beckoned to me in my dream, inviting me to join her, but I remained standing on the veranda steps until she danced away into the distance and faded from view.

And in the morning when I woke I found a red rose, moist with dew, lying beside my pillow.

Ruskin Bond

on fairy hill

Those little green lights that I used to see twinkling away on Pari Tibba—there had to be a scientific explanation for them. I was sure of that. After dark we see or hear many things that seem mysterious and irrational. And then, by the clear light of day, we find that the magic and the mystery have an explanation after all.

I saw those lights occasionally, late at night, when I walked home from the town to my little cottage at the edge of the forest. They moved too fast to be torches or lanterns carried by people. And as there were no roads on Pari Tibba, they could not have been cycle or cart lamps. Someone told me there was phosphorus in the rocks and that this probably accounted for the luminous glow emanating from the hillside late at night. Possibly, but I was not convinced.

My encounter with the little people happened by the light of day.

One morning early in April, purely on an impulse, I decided to climb to the top of Pari Tibba and look around for myself. It was springtime in the Himalayan foothills. The sap was rising—in the trees, in the grass, in the wildflowers, in my own veins. I took the path through the oak forest, down to the little stream at the foot of the hill, and then up the steep slope of Pari Tibba, Hill of Fairies.

It was quite a scramble to get to the top. The path ended at the stream at the bottom of the slope. I had to clutch at brambles and tufts of grass to make the ascent. Fallen pine needles, slippery underfoot, made it difficult to get a foothold. But finally I made it to the top—a grassy plateau fringed by pines and a few wild medlar trees now clothed in white blossom.

It was a pretty spot. And as I was hot and sweaty, I removed most of my clothing and lay down under a medlar to rest. The climb had been quite tiring. But a fresh breeze soon revived me. It made a soft humming sound in the pines. And the grass, sprinkled with yellow buttercups, buzzed with the sound of crickets and grasshoppers.

After some time, I stood up and surveyed the scene. To the north, Landour with its rusty red-roofed cottages; to the south, the wide valley and a silver stream flowing towards the Ganga. To the west were rolling hills, patches of forest and a small village tucked into a fold of the mountain.

Disturbed by my presence, a barking deer ran across the clearing and down the opposite slope. A band of long-tailed blue magpies rose from the oak trees, glided across the knoll, and settled in another copse of oaks.

I was alone, alone with the wind and the sky. It had probably been months, possibly years, since any human had passed that way. The soft lush grass looked most inviting. I lay down again on the sun-warmed sward. Pressed and bruised by my weight, the catmint and clover in the grass gave out a soft fragrance. A ladybird climbed up my leg and began to explore my body. A swarm of white butterflies fluttered around me.

I slept.

I have no idea how long I slept. When I awoke, it was to experience an unusual soothing sensation all over my limbs, as though they were being gently stroked with rose petals.

All lethargy gone, I opened my eyes to find a little girl—or was it a woman?—about two inches tall, sitting cross-legged on my chest and studying me intently. Her hair fell in long black tresses. Her skin was the colour of honey. Her firm little breasts were like tiny acorns. She held a buttercup, which was larger than her hand, and she was stroking my skin with it.

I was tingling all over. A sensation of sensual joy surged through my limbs.

A tiny boy—man?—also naked, now joined the elfin girl, and they held hands and looked into my eyes, smiling. Their teeth were like little pearls, their lips soft petals of apricot blossom. Were these the nature spirits, the flower fairies, I had often dreamt of?

I raised my head, and saw that there were scores of little people all over me. The delicate and gentle creatures were exploring my legs, arms and body with caressing gestures. Some of them were laving me with dew or pollen or some other soft essence. I closed my eyes again. Waves of pure physical pleasure swept over me. I had never known anything like it. It was endless, all-embracing. My limbs turned to water. The sky revolved around me, and I must have fainted.

When I came to, perhaps an hour later, the little people had gone. The fragrance of honeysuckle lingered in the air. A deep rumble overhead made me look up. Dark clouds had gathered, threatening rain. Had the thunder frightened them away to their abode beneath the rocks and roots? Or had they simply tired of sporting with an unknown newcomer? Mischievous they were; for when I looked around for my clothes I could not find them anywhere.

A wave of panic surged over me. I ran here and there, looking behind shrubs and tree trunks, but to no avail. My clothes had disappeared, along with the fairies—if indeed they were fairies!

It began to rain. Large drops cannoned off the dry rocks. Then it hailed, and soon the slope was covered with ice. There was no shelter. Naked, I clambered down as far as the stream. There was no one to see me—except for a wild mountain goat speeding away in the opposite direction. Gusts of wind slashed rain and hail across my face and body. Panting and shivering, I took shelter beneath an overhanging rock until the storm had passed. By then it was almost dusk, and I was able to ascend the path to my cottage without encountering anyone, apart from a band of startled langurs who chattered excitedly on seeing me.

I couldn't stop shivering, so I went straight to bed. I slept a deep dreamless sleep through the afternoon, evening and night, and woke up next morning with a high fever.

Mechanically I dressed, made myself some breakfast and tried to get through the morning's chores. When I took my temperature, I found it was 104. So I swallowed a Brufen and went back to bed.

There I lay till late afternoon, when the postman's knocking woke me. I left my letters unopened on my desk—breaking a sacrosanct ritual—and returned to my bed.

The fever lasted almost a week and left me weak and feeble. I couldn't have climbed Pari Tibba again even if I'd wanted to. But I reclined on my window seat and looked at the clouds drifting over that bleak hill. Desolate it seemed, and yet strangely inhabited. When it grew dark, I waited for those little green fairy lights to appear; but these, it seemed, were now to be denied to me.

And so I returned to my desk, my typewriter, my newspaper articles and correspondence. It was a lonely period in my life. My marriage hadn't worked out: my wife, fond of high society and averse to living with an unsuccessful writer in a remote cottage in the woods, was pursuing her own, more successful career in Mumbai. I had always been rather half-hearted in my approach to making money, whereas she had always wanted more and more of it. She left me—left me with my books and my dreams . . .

Had it all been a dream, that strange episode on Pari Tibba? Had a too-active imagination conjured up those aerial spirits, those *siddhas* of the upper air? Or were they underground people, living deep within the bowels of the hill? If I was going to preserve my sanity, I knew I had better get on with the more mundane aspects of living—going into town to buy groceries, mending the leaking roof, paying the electricity bill, plodding up to the post office, and remembering to deposit the odd cheque that came my way. All the routine things that made life so dull and dreary.

The truth is, what we commonly call life is not really living at all. The regular and settled ways which we accept as the course of life are really the curse of life. They tie us down to the trivial and monotonous, and we will do almost anything to get away, ideally for a more exalted and fulfilling existence, but if that is not possible, for a few hours of forgetfulness in alcohol, drugs, forbidden sex or even golf. So it would give me great joy to go underground with the fairies. Those little people who have sought refuge in Mother Earth from mankind's killing ways are as vulnerable as butterflies and flowers. All things beautiful are easily destroyed.

I am sitting at my window in the gathering dark, penning these stray thoughts, when I see them coming—hand-in-hand, walking on a swirl of mist, suffused with all the radiant colours of the rainbow. For a rainbow has formed a bridge for them from Pari Tibba to the edge of my window.

I am ready to go with them to their secret lairs or to the upper air—far from the stifling confines of the world in which we toil . . .

Come, fairies, carry me away, to experience again the perfection I did that summer's day!

fourteen

would astley return?

The house was called Undercliff because that's where it stood—under a cliff. The man who went away—the owner of the house—was Robert Astley. And the man who stayed behind—the old family retainer—was Prem Bahadur.

Astley had been gone many years. He was still a bachelor in his late thirties when he'd suddenly decided that he wanted adventure, romance and faraway places. And he'd given the keys of the house to Prem Bahadur—who'd served the family for thirty years—and had set off on his travels.

Someone saw him in Sri Lanka. He'd been heard of in Burma around the ruby mines at Mogok. Then he turned up in Java seeking a passage through the Sunda Straits. After that the trail petered out. Years passed. The house in the hill station remained empty.

But Prem Bahadur was still there, living in an outhouse.

Every day he opened up Undercliff, dusted the furniture in all the rooms, made sure that the bedsheets and pillowcases were clean and set out Astley's dressing-gown and slippers.

In the old days, whenever Astley had come home after a journey or a long tramp in the hills, he had liked to bathe and change into his gown and slippers, no matter what the hour. Prem Bahadur still kept them ready. He was convinced that Robert would return one day.

Astley himself had said so.

'Keep everything ready for me, Prem, old chap. I may be back after a year, or two years, or even longer, but I'll be back, I promise you. On the first of every month I want you to go to my lawyer, Mr Kapoor. He'll give you your salary and any money that's needed for the rates and repairs. I want you to keep the house tip-top!'

'Will you bring back a wife, sahib?'

'Lord, no! Whatever put that idea in your head?'

'I thought, perhaps—because you wanted

the house kept ready . . .'

'Ready for me, Prem. I don't want to come home and find the old place falling down.'

And so Prem had taken care of the house—although there was no news from Astley. What had happened to him? The mystery provided a talking-point whenever local people met on the Mall. And in the bazaar the shopkeepers missed Astley because he had been a man who spent freely.

His relatives still believed him to be alive. Only a few months back a brother had turned up—a brother who had a farm in Canada and could not stay in India for long. He had deposited a further sum with the lawyer and told Prem to carry on as before. The salary provided Prem with his few needs. Moreover, he was convinced that Robert would return.

Another man might have neglected the house and grounds, but not Prem Bahadur. He had a genuine regard for the absent owner. Prem was much older—now almost sixty and none too strong, suffering from pleurisy and other chest troubles—but he remembered Robert as both a boy and a young man. They had been together on numerous hunting and fishing trips in the mountains. They had slept out under the stars, bathed in icy mountain streams, and eaten from the same cooking-pot. Once, when crossing a small river, they had been swept downstream by a flash flood, a wall of water that came thundering down the gorges without any warning during the rainy season. Together they had struggled back to safety. Back in the hill station, Astley told everyone that Prem had saved his life while Prem was equally insistent that he owed his life to Robert.

This year the monsoon had begun early and ended late. It dragged on through most of September and Prem Bahadur's cough grew worse and his breathing more difficult.

He lay on his charpai on the veranda, staring out at the garden, which was beginning to get out of hand, a tangle of dahlias, snake-lilies and convolvulus. The sun finally came out. The wind shifted from the south-west to the north-west and swept the clouds away.

Prem Bahadur had shifted his charpai into the garden and was lying in the sun, puffing at his small hookah, when he saw Robert Astley at the gate.

He tried to get up but his legs would not oblige him. The hookah slipped from his hand.

Astley came walking down the garden path and stopped in front of the old retainer, smiling

Ruskin Bond

down at him. He did not look a day older than when Prem Bahadur had last seen him.

'So you have come at last,' said Prem.

'I told you I'd return.'

'It has been many years. But you have not changed.'

'Nor have you, old chap.'

'I have grown old and sick and feeble.'

'You'll be fine now. That's why I've come.'

'I'll open the house,' said Prem and this time he found himself getting up quite easily.

'It isn't necessary,' said Astley.

'But all is ready for you!'

'I know. I have heard of how well you have looked after everything. Come then, let's take a last look around. We cannot stay, you know.'

Prem was a little mystified but he opened the front door and took Robert through the drawing-room and up the stairs to the bedroom. Robert saw the dressing-gown and the slippers and he placed his hand gently on the old man's shoulder.

When they returned downstairs and emerged into the sunlight Prem was surprised to see himself—or rather his skinny body—stretched out on the charpai. The hookah was on the ground, where it had fallen.

Prem looked at Astley in bewilderment.

'But who is that—lying there?'

'It was you. Only the husk now, the empty shell. This is the real you, standing here beside me.'

'You came for me?'

'I couldn't come until you were ready. As for me, I left *my* shell a long time ago. But you were determined to hang on, keeping this house together. Are you ready now?'

'And the house?'

'Others will live in it. But come, it's time to go fishing . . .'

Astley took Prem by the arm, and they walked through the dappled sunlight under the deodars and finally left that place for ever.

fifteen

the prize

They were up late, drinking in the old Ritz bar, and by one a.m. everyone was pretty well sloshed. Ganesh got into his electric blue Zen and zigzagged home. Victor drove off in his antique Morris Minor, which promptly broke down, forcing him to transfer to a taxi. Nandu, the proprietor, limped off to his cottage, a shooting pain in his foot presaging another attack of gout. Begum Tara, who had starred in over a hundred early talkies, climbed into a cycle rickshaw that had no driver, which hardly mattered as she promptly fell asleep. The bartender vanished into the night. Only Rahul, the romantic young novelist, remained in the foyer, wondering where everyone had gone and why he had been left behind.

The rooms were full. There wasn't a spare bed in the hotel, for it was the height of the season and the hill station's hotels were overflowing. The room boys and kitchen staff had gone to their quarters. Only the night chowkidar's whistle could occasionally be heard as the retired havildar prowled around the estate.

The young writer felt he had been unfairly abandoned, and rather resented the slight. He'd been the life and soul of the party—or so he'd thought—telling everyone about the huge advance he'd just got for his latest book and how it was a certainty for the Booker Prize. He hadn't noticed their yawns; or if he had, he'd put it down to the lack of oxygen in the bar. It had been named the Horizontal Bar by one of the patrons, because of a tendency on the part of some of the clientele to fall asleep on the carpet—that very same carpet on which the Duke of Savoy had passed out exactly a hundred years ago.

Rahul had no intention of passing out on the floor. But his libations had made lying down somewhere seem quite imperative. A billiard table would have been fine, but the billiard room was locked. He staggered down the corridor; not a sofa or easy chair came into

Ruskin Bond

view. Finally, he found a door that opened, leading to the huge empty dining room, now lit only by a single electric bulb.

The old piano did not look too inviting, but the long dining table had been cleared of everything except a curry-stained tablecloth left there to do duty again at breakfast. Rahul managed to hoist himself up on the table and stretch himself out. It made a hard bed, and already stray breadcrumbs were irritating his tender skin, but he was too tired to care. The light bulb directly above him also failed to bother him too much. Although there was no air in the room, the bulb swayed slightly, as though an invisible hand had tapped it gently.

For an hour he slept, a deep dreamless sleep, and then he became vaguely aware of music, voices, footsteps and laughter. Someone was playing the piano. Chairs were pulled back. Glasses tinkled. Knives and forks clattered against dinner plates.

Rahul opened his eyes to find a banquet in progress. On *his* table—the table he was lying on—now flanked by huge tureens of food! And the diners were seemingly unaware of his presence. The men wore old-fashioned dress suits with bow ties and high collars; the women wore long flounced dresses with tight bodices that showed their ample bosoms to good advantage. Out of long habit, Rahul's hand automatically reached out for the nearest breast, and for once he did not receive a stinging slap; for the simple reason that his hands, if they were there at all, hadn't moved.

Someone said, 'Roast pig—I've been looking forward to this!' and stuck a knife and fork into Rahul's thigh.

He cried out, or tried to, but no one heard; he could not hear his own voice. He found he could raise his head and look down the length of his body, and he saw he had pig's trotters instead of his own feet.

Someone turned him over and sliced a bit off his rump.

'A most tender leg of pork,' remarked a woman on his left.

A fork jabbed him in the buttocks. Then a giant of a man, top-hatted, with a carving knife in his hand, leant over him. He wore a broad white apron, and on it was written in large letters CHAIRMAN OF THE JURY. The carving knife glistened in the lamplight.

Rahul screamed and leapt off the table. He fell against the piano, recovered his balance, dashed past the revellers, and out of the vast dining room.

He ran down the silent hotel corridor, banging on all the doors. But none opened to him. Finally, at Room No. 12A—hotels do not like using the number 13—the door gave way. Out of breath, shaking all over, our hero stumbled into the room and bolted the door behind him.

It was a single room with a single bed. The bedclothes appeared to be in some disarray but Rahul hardly noticed. All he wanted was to end the nightmare he had been having and get some sleep. Kicking off his shoes, he climbed into the bed fully dressed.

He had been lying there for at least five minutes before he realized that he wasn't alone in the bed. There was someone lying beside him, covered by a sheet. Rahul switched on the bedside lamp. Nothing moved, the body lay still. On the sheet, in large letters, were the words: BETTER LUCK NEXT TIME.

He pulled the sheet back and stared down at his own dead self.

eyes of the cat

Her eyes seemed flecked with gold when the sun was on them. And as the sun set over the mountains, drawing a deep red wound across the sky, there was more than gold in Kiran's eyes. There was anger; for she had been cut to the quick by some remarks her teacher had made—the culmination of weeks of insults and taunts.

Kiran was poorer than most of the girls in her class and could not afford the tuitions that had become almost obligatory if one was to pass and be promoted. 'You'll have to spend another year in the ninth,' said Madam. 'And if you don't like that, you can find another school—a school where it won't matter if your blouse is torn and your tunic is old and your shoes are falling apart.' Madam had shown her large teeth in what was supposed to be a good-natured smile, and all the girls had tittered dutifully. Sycophancy had become part of the curriculum in Madam's private academy for girls.

On the way home in the gathering gloom, Kiran's two companions commiserated with her.

'She's a mean old thing,' said Aarti. 'She doesn't care for anyone but herself.'

'Her laugh reminds me of a donkey braying,' said Sunita, who was more forthright.

But Kiran wasn't really listening. Her eyes were fixed on some point in the far distance, where the pines stood in silhouette against a night sky that was growing brighter every moment. The moon was rising, a full moon, a moon that meant something very special to Kiran, that made her blood tingle and her skin prickle and her hair glow and send out sparks. Her steps seemed to grow lighter, her limbs more sinewy as she moved gracefully, softly over the mountain path.

Abruptly she left her companions at a fork in the road.

'I'm taking the short cut through the forest,' she said.

Her friends were used to her sudden whims. They knew she was not afraid of being alone in the dark. But Kiran's moods made them feel a little nervous, and now, holding hands, they hurried home along the open road.

The short cut took Kiran through the dark oak forest. The crooked, tormented branches of the oaks threw twisted shadows across the path. A jackal howled at the moon; a nightjar called from the bushes. Kiran walked fast, not out of fear but from urgency, and her breath came in short, sharp gasps. Bright moonlight bathed the hillside when she reached her home on the outskirts of the village.

Refusing her dinner, she went straight to her small room and flung the window open. Moonbeams crept over the window-sill and over her arms which were already covered with golden hair. Her strong nails had shredded the rotten wood of the window-sill.

Tail swishing and ears pricked, the tawny leopard came swiftly out of the window, crossed the open field behind the house, and melted into the shadows.

A little later it padded silently through the forest.

Although the moon shone brightly on the

tin-roofed town, the leopard knew where the shadows were deepest and merged beautifully with them. An occasional intake of breath, which resulted in a short rasping cough, was the only sound it made.

Madam was returning from dinner at a ladies' club, called the Kitten Club as a sort of foil to the husbands' club affiliations. There were still a few people in the street, and while no one could help noticing Madam, who had the contours of a steam-roller, none saw or heard the predator who had slipped down a side alley and reached the steps of the teacher's house. It sat there silently, waiting with all the patience of an obedient schoolgirl.

When Madam saw the leopard on her steps, she dropped her handbag and opened her mouth to scream; but her voice would not materialize. Nor would her tongue ever be used again, either to savour chicken biryani or to pour scorn upon her pupils, for the leopard had sprung at her throat, broken her neck, and dragged her into the bushes.

In the morning, when Aarti and Sunita set out for school, they stopped as usual at Kiran's cottage and called out to her.

Kiran was sitting in the sun, combing her

long black hair.

'Aren't you coming to school today, Kiran?' asked the girls.

'No, I won't bother to go today,' said Kiran. She felt lazy, but pleased with herself, like a contented cat.

'Madam won't be pleased,' said Aarti. 'Shall we tell her you're sick?'

'It won't be necessary,' said Kiran, and gave them one of her mysterious smiles. 'I'm sure it's going to be a holiday.'

Ruskin Bond

susanna's seven
husbands

Locally the tomb was known as 'the grave of the seven times married one.'

You'd be forgiven for thinking it was Bluebeard's grave; he was reputed to have killed several wives in turn because they showed undue curiosity about a locked room. But this was the tomb of Susanna Anna-Maria Yeates, and the inscription (most of it in Latin) stated that she was mourned by all who had benefited from her generosity, her beneficiaries having included various schools, orphanages, and the church across the road. There was no sign of any other graves in the vicinity and presumably her husbands had been interred in the old Rajpur graveyard, below the Delhi Ridge.

I was still in my teens when I first saw the ruins of what had once been a spacious and handsome mansion. Desolate and silent, its well-laid paths were overgrown with weeds, and its flower beds had disappeared under a growth of thorny jungle. The two-storeyed house had looked across the Grand Trunk Road. Now abandoned, feared and shunned, it stood encircled in mystery, reputedly the home of evil spirits.

Outside the gate, along the Grand Trunk Road, thousands of vehicles sped by—cars, trucks, buses, tractors, bullock carts—but few noticed the old mansion or its mausoleum, set back as they were from the main road, hidden by mango, neem and peepal trees. One old and massive peepal tree grew out of the ruins of the house, strangling it much as its owner was said to have strangled, one of her dispensable paramours.

As a much-married person with a quaint habit of disposing of her husbands whenever she tired of them, Susanna's malignant spirit was said to haunt the deserted garden. I had examined the tomb, I had gazed upon the ruins, I had scrambled through shrubbery and overgrown rose bushes, but I had not encountered the spirit of this mysterious woman.

Ruskin Bond

Perhaps, at the time, I was too pure and innocent to be targeted by malignant spirits. For malignant she must have been, if the stories about her were true.

The vaults of the ruined mansion were rumoured to contain a buried treasure—the amassed wealth of the lady Susanna. But no one dared go down there, for the vaults were said to be occupied by a family of cobras, traditional guardians of buried treasure. Had she really been a woman of great wealth, and could treasure still be buried there? I put these questions to Naushad, the furniture-maker, who had lived in the vicinity all his life, and whose father had made the furniture and fittings for this and other great houses in Old Delhi.

'Lady Susanna, as she was known, was much sought after for her wealth,' recalled Naushad. 'She was no miser, either. She spent freely, reigning in state in her palatial home, with many horses and carriages at her disposal. Every evening she rode through the Roshanara Gardens, the cynosure of all eyes, for she was beautiful as well as wealthy. Yes, all men sought her favours, and she could choose from the best of them. Many were fortune hunters. She did not discourage them. Some found favour for a time, but she soon tired of them. None of her husbands enjoyed her wealth for very long!

'Today no one enters those ruins, where once there was mirth and laughter. She was the Zamindari lady, the owner of much land, and she administered her estate with a strong hand. She was kind if rents were paid when they fell due, but terrible if someone failed to pay.

'Well, over fifty years have gone by since she was laid to rest, but still men speak of her with awe. Her spirit is restless, and it is said that she often visits the scenes of her former splendour. She has been seen walking through this gate, or riding in the gardens, or driving in her phaeton down the Rajpur road.'

'And what happened to all those husbands?' I asked.

'Most of them died mysterious deaths. Even the doctors were baffled. Tomkins sahib drank too much. The lady soon tired of him. A drunken husband is a burdensome creature, she was heard to say. He would eventually have drunk himself to death, but she was an impatient woman and was anxious to replace him. You see those datura bushes growing wild in the grounds? They have always done well here.'

'Belladonna?' I suggested.

'That's right, huzoor. Introduced in the whisky-soda, it put him to sleep for ever.'

'She was quite humane in her way.'

'Oh, very humane, sir. She hated to see anyone suffer. One sahib, I don't know his name, drowned in the tank behind the house, where the water lilies grew. But she made sure he was half-dead before he fell in. She had large, powerful hands, they said.'

'Why did she bother to marry them? Couldn't she just have had men friends?'

'Not in those days, huzoor. Respectable society would not have tolerated it. Neither in India nor in the West would it have been permitted.'

'She was born out of her time,' I remarked.

'True, sir. And remember, most of them were fortune hunters. So we need not waste too much pity on them.'

'*She* did not waste any.'

'She was without pity. Especially when she found out what they were really after. Snakes had a better chance of survival.'

'How did the other husbands take their leave of this world?'

'Well, the Colonel sahib shot himself while cleaning his rifle. Purely an accident, huzoor. Although some say she had loaded his gun without his knowledge. Such was her reputation by now that she was suspected even when innocent. But she bought her way out of trouble. It was easy enough, if you were wealthy.'

'And the fourth husband?'

'Oh, he died a natural death. There was a cholera epidemic that year, and he was carried off by the *haija*. Although, again, there were some who said that a good dose of arsenic produced the same symptoms! Anyway it was cholera on the death certificate. And the doctor who signed it was the next to marry her.'

'Being a doctor, he was probably quite careful about what he ate and drank.'

'He lasted about a year.'

'What happened?'

'He was bitten by a cobra.'

'Well, that was just bad luck, wasn't it? You could hardly blame it on Susanna.'

'No, huzoor, but the cobra was in his bedroom. It was coiled around the bedpost. And when he undressed for the night, it struck! He was dead when Susanna came into the room an hour later. She had a way with snakes. She did not harm them and they never attacked her.'

'And there were no antidotes in those days. Exit the doctor. Who was the sixth husband?'

'A handsome man. An indigo planter. He had gone bankrupt when the indigo trade came to an end. He was hoping to recover his fortune with the good lady's help. But our Susanna mem, she did not believe in sharing her fortune with anyone.'

'How did she remove the indigo planter?'

'It was said that she lavished strong drink upon him, and when he lay helpless, she assisted him on the road we all have to take by pouring molten lead in his ears.'

'A painless death, I'm told.'

'But a terrible price to pay, huzoor, simply because one is no longer needed . . .'

We walked along the dusty highway, enjoying the evening breeze, and some time later we entered the Roshanara Gardens, in those days Delhi's most popular and fashionable meeting place.

'You have told me how six of her husbands died, Naushad. I thought there were seven?'

'Ah the seventh was a gallant young magistrate who perished right here, huzoor. They were driving through the park after dark when the lady's carriage was attacked by brigands. In defending her, the young man received a fatal sword wound.'

'Not the lady's fault, Naushad.'

'No, huzoor. But he was a magistrate, remember, and the assailants, one of whose relatives had been convicted by him, were out for revenge. Oddly enough, though, two of the men were given employment by the lady Susanna at a later date. You may draw your own conclusions.'

'And were there others?'

'Not husbands. But an adventurer, a soldier of fortune came along. He found her treasure, they say. And he lies buried with it, in the cellars of the ruined house. His bones lie scattered there, among gold and silver and precious jewels. The cobras guard them still! But how he perished was a mystery, and remains so till this day.'

'And Susanna? What happened to her?'

'She lived to a ripe old age. If she paid for her crimes, it wasn't in this life! She had no children, but she started an orphanage and gave generously to the poor and to various schools and institutions, including a home for widows. She died peacefully in her sleep.'

'A merry widow,' I remarked. 'The Black Widow spider!'

Don't go looking for Susanna's tomb. It vanished some years ago, along with the ruins of her mansion. A smart new housing estate came up on the site, but not after several workmen and a contractor succumbed to snake bite! Occasionally residents complain of a malignant ghost in their midst, who is given to flagging down cars, especially those driven by single men. There have also been one or two mysterious disappearances.

And after dusk, an old-fashioned horse and carriage can sometimes be seen driven through the Roshanara Gardens. If you chance upon it, ignore it, my friend. Don't stop to answer any questions from the beautiful fair lady who smiles at you from behind lace curtains. She's still looking for her final victim.

eighteen

the trouble with jinns

My friend Jimmy has only one arm. He lost the other when he was a young man of twenty-five. The story of how he lost his good right arm is a little difficult to believe, but I swear that it is absolutely true.

To begin with, Jimmy was (and presumably still is) a Jinn. Now a Jinn isn't really a human like us. A Jinn is a spirit creature from another world who has assumed, for a lifetime, the physical aspect of a human being. Jimmy was a true Jinn and he had the Jinn's gift of being able to elongate his arm at will. Most Jinns can stretch their arms to a distance of twenty or thirty feet. Jimmy could attain forty feet. His arm would move through space or up walls or along the ground like a beautiful gliding serpent.

I have seen him stretched out beneath a mango tree, helping himself to ripe mangoes from the top of the tree. He loved mangoes. He was a natural glutton and it was probably his gluttony that first led time to misuse his peculiar gifts.

We were at school together at a hill station in northern India. Jimmy was particularly good at basketball. He was clever enough not to lengthen his arm too much because he did not want anyone to know that he was a Jinn. In the boxing ring he generally won his fights. His opponents never seemed to get past his amazing reach. He just kept tapping them on the nose until they retired from the ring bloody and bewildered.

It was during the half-term examinations that I stumbled on Jimmy's secret. We had been set a particularly difficult algebra paper but I had managed to cover a couple of sheets with correct answers and was about to forge ahead on another sheet when I noticed someone's hand on my desk. At first I thought it was the invigilator's. But when I looked up there was no one beside me. Could it be the boy sitting directly behind? No, he was engrossed in his question paper and had his hands to himself. Meanwhile, the hand on my desk had grasped my answer-sheets and was cautiously moving off. Following its descent, I found that it was attached to an arm of amazing length and pliability. This moved stealthily down the desk and slithered across the floor, shrinking all the while, until it was restored to its normal length. Its owner was of course one who had never been any good at algebra.

I had to write out my answers a second time but after the exam I went straight up to Jimmy, told him I didn't like his game and threatened to expose him. He begged me not to let anyone know, assured me that he couldn't really help himself, and offered to be of service to me whenever I wished. It was tempting to have Jimmy as my friend, for with his long reach he would obviously be useful. I agreed to overlook the matter of the pilfered papers and we became the best of pals.

It did not take me long to discover that Jimmy's gift was more of a nuisance than a constructive aid. That was because Jimmy had a second-rate mind and did not know how to make proper use of his powers. He seldom rose above the trivial. He used his long arm in the tuck-shop, in the classroom, in the dormitory. And when we were allowed out to the cinema, he used it in the dark of the hall.

Now the trouble with all Jinns is that they

have a weakness for women with long black hair. The longer and blacker the hair, the better for Jinns. And should a Jinn manage to take possession of the woman he desires, she goes into a decline and her beauty decays. Everything about her is destroyed except for the beautiful long black hair.

Jimmy was still too young to be able to take possession in this way, but he couldn't resist touching and stroking long black hair. The cinema was the best place for the indulgence of his whims. His arm would start stretching, his fingers would feel their way along the rows of seats, and his lengthening limb would slowly work its way along the aisle until it reached the back of the seat in which sat the object of his admiration. His hand would stroke the long black hair with great tenderness and if the girl felt anything and looked round, Jimmy's hand would disappear behind the seat and lie there poised like the hood of a snake, ready to strike again.

At college two or three years later, Jimmy's first real victim succumbed to his attentions. She was a lecturer in Economics, not very good-looking, but her hair, black and lustrous, reached almost to her knees. She usually kept it in plaits but Jimmy saw her one morning, just after she had taken a head-bath, and her hair lay spread out on the cot on which she was reclining. Jimmy could no longer control himself. His spirit, the very essence of his personality, entered the woman's body and the next day she was distraught, feverish and excited. She would not eat, went into a coma, and in a few days dwindled to a mere skeleton. When she died, she was nothing but skin and bone but her hair had lost none of its loveliness.

I took pains to avoid Jimmy after this tragic event. I could not prove that he was the cause of the lady's sad demise but in my own heart I was quite certain of it. For, since meeting Jimmy, I had read a good deal about Jinns and knew their ways.

We did not see each other for a few years. And then, holidaying in the hills last year, I found we were staying at the same hotel. I could not very well ignore him and after we had drunk a few beers together I began to feel that I had perhaps misjudged Jimmy and that he was not the irresponsible Jinn I had taken him for. Perhaps the college lecturer had died of some mysterious malady that attacks only college lecturers and Jimmy had nothing at all to do with it.

We had decided to take our lunch and a

few bottles of beer to a grassy knoll just below the main motor-road. It was late afternoon and I had been sleeping off the effects of the beer when I woke to find Jimmy looking rather agitated.

'What's wrong?' I asked.

'Up there, under the pine trees,' he said. 'Just above the road. Don't you see them?'

'I see two girls,' I said. 'So what?'

'The one on the left. Haven't you noticed her hair?'

'Yes, it is very long and beautiful and—now look, Jimmy, you'd better get a grip on yourself.' But already his hand was out of sight, his arm snaking up the hillside and across the road.

Presently I saw the hand emerge from some bushes near the girls and then cautiously make its way to the girl with the black tresses. So absorbed was Jimmy in the pursuit of his favourite pastime that he failed to hear the blowing of a horn. Around the bend of the road came a speeding Mercedes-Benz truck.

Jimmy saw the truck but there wasn't time for him to shrink his arm back to normal. It lay right across the entire width of the road and when the truck had passed over it, it writhed and twisted like a mortally wounded python.

By the time the truck-driver and I could fetch a doctor, the arm (or what was left of it) had shrunk to its ordinary size. We took Jimmy to hospital where, the doctors found it necessary to amputate. The truck-driver, who kept insisting that the arm he ran over was at least thirty feet long, was arrested on a charge of drunken driving.

Some weeks later I asked Jimmy, 'Why are you so depressed? You still have one arm. Isn't it gifted in the same way?'

'I never tried to find out,' he said, 'and I'm not going to try now.'

He is of course still a Jinn at heart and whenever he sees a girl with long black hair he must be terribly tempted to try out his one good arm and stroke her beautiful tresses. But he has learnt his lesson. It is better to be a human without any gifts than a Jinn or a genius with one too many.

nineteen

the haunted bungalow

It was Grandmother who decided that we must move house.

And it was all because of a *pret*, a mischievous ghost who had been making life intolerable for everyone.

*Pret*s usually live in peepal trees, and that's where our *pret* first had his abode—in the branches of an old peepal which had grown through the compound wall and had spread into the garden, on one side, and over the road, on the other.

For many years the *pret* had lived there quite happily, without bothering anyone in the house. I suppose the traffic on the road had kept him fully occupied. Sometimes, when a tonga was passing, he would frighten the pony, and as a result the little pony-cart would go careening off in the wrong direction. Occasionally he would get into the engine of a car or bus, which would have a breakdown soon after. And he liked to knock the sola-topis off the heads of Sahibs, who would curse and wonder how a breeze had sprung up so suddenly, only to die down again just as quickly. Although the *pret* could make himself felt, and sometimes heard, he was invisible to the human eye.

At night people avoided walking beneath the peepal tree. It was said that if you yawned beneath the tree, the *pret* would jump down your throat and ruin your digestion. Our gardener, Manphool, who was always talking taking sick-leave, blamed the *pret* for all his tummy-troubles. Once, when yawning, Manphool had forgotten to snap his fingers in front of his mouth, and the *pret* had got in without any difficulty.

But it had left us alone until, one day, the peepal tree was cut down.

It wasn't our fault, except of course that Grandfather had given the PWD permission to cut the tree, which had been on our land. They wanted to widen the road, and the tree and a bit of our wall was in the way; so both had to go. In any case, not even a ghost can prevail against the PWD.

But hardly a day had passed when we discovered that the *pret*, deprived of his tree, had decided to take up residence in the bungalow.

And since a good *pret* must be bad in order to justify his existence, it was not long before he was up to all sorts of mischief in the house.

He began by hiding Grandmother's spectacles whenever she took them off.

'I'm sure I put them down on the dressing table,' she grumbled.

A little later they were found balanced precariously on the snout of a wild boar, whose stuffed and mounted head adorned the veranda wall. Being the only boy in the house, I was at first blamed for this prank; but a day or two later, when the spectacles disappeared again only to be discovered dangling from the bars of the parrot's cage, it was agreed that some other agency was at work.

Grandfather was the next to be troubled. He went into the garden one morning to find all his prize sweetpeas snipped off and lying on the ground. Uncle Ken maintained that the red-vented bulbuls had destroyed the flowers, but we didn't think the birds could have finished off all the blooms just before sunrise.

Uncle Ken himself was soon to suffer. He was a heavy sleeper, and once he'd gone to bed he hated being woken up. So when he came to the breakfast table looking bleary-eyed and miserable, we asked him if he was feeling all right.

'I couldn't sleep a wink last night,' he complained. 'Every time I was about to fall asleep, the bedclothes would be pulled off the bed. I had to get up at least a dozen times to pick them off the floor.' He stared balefully at me. 'Where were *you* sleeping last night, young man?'

'In Grandfather's room,' I said.

'That's right,' said Grandfather. 'And I'm a light sleeper. I'd have woken up if he'd been sleep-walking.'

'It's that ghost from the peepal tree,' said Grandmother decisively. 'It's moved into the house. First my spectacles, then the sweetpeas, and now Ken's bedclothes! What will it be up to next, I wonder?'

We did not have to wonder for long. There followed a week of disasters. Vases fell off tables, pictures fell from walls. Parrot's feathers turned up in the teapot while the parrot himself let out indignant squawks in the middle of the

Ruskin Bond

night. Windows which had been closed would be found open, and open windows closed. Uncle Ken found a crow's nest in his bed, and on tossing it out of the window was attacked by two crows.

When Aunt Mabel came to stay, things got worse. The *pret* seemed to take an immediate dislike to Aunt Mabel. She was a nervous, excitable person, just the right sort of prey for a spiteful ghost. Somehow her toothpaste got switched with a tube of Grandfather's shaving-cream; and when she appeared in the sitting-room, foaming at the mouth, we ran for our lives, Uncle Ken shouting that she'd got rabies.

Two days later Aunt Mabel complained that she had been hit on the nose by a grapefruit, which had leapt inexplicably from the pantry shelf and hurtled across the room at her. A bruised and swollen nose testified to the attack.

'We'll have to leave the house,' said Grandmother. 'If we stay here much longer, both Ken and Mabel will get nervous breakdowns.'

'I thought Aunt Mabel broke down long ago,' I said.

'None of your cheek,' snapped Aunt Mabel.

'Anyway, I agree about changing the house.' I said breezily. 'I can't even do my homework. The ink-bottle is always empty.'

'There was ink in the soup last night,' complained Uncle Ken.

'We'll have to move, I suppose,' said Grandfather, 'even if it's only for a couple of months. Perhaps the ghost will go away. There's my brother's house in Barlowganj. He won't be using it for a few months. We'll move in next week.'

And so, a few days and several disasters later, we began moving house.

The bullock-carts laden with furniture and heavy luggage were sent ahead. The roof of our old Ford was piled high with bags and kitchen utensils. All of us managed to squeeze into the car; Grandfather taking the wheel.

We were barely out of the gate when we heard a peculiar sound, as of someone chuckling and talking to himself, coming from the roof of the car.

'Is the parrot out there on the luggage-rack?' asked Grandfather.

'No,' said Grandmother, 'he's with Manphool on a bullock-cart.'

Grandfather stopped the car, got out, and took a look at the roof.

'Nothing up there,' he said, getting in and starting the engine. 'I thought I heard the parrot talking.'

Ruskin Bond

Grandfather had driven us a few furlongs along the road when the chuckling started again, followed by a squeaky little voice chattering in fluent Hindustani. We all heard it and understood what it was saying. It was the *pret* talking to himself.

'*Chalo*—let's go!' it exclaimed gleefully. '*Naya ghar*—a new house! *Kya maza aiga* . . . what fun I'm going to have!'

twenty

ganpat's story

The beggars on the whole are a thriving community and it came as no surprise to me when the municipality decided to place a tax on begging.

I know that some beggars earned, on an average, more than a chaprasi or a clerk. I knew for certain that the one-legged man, who had been hobbling about town on crutches long before I came to Pipalnagar, sent money orders home every month. Begging had become a profession, and so perhaps the municipality felt justified in taxing it and, besides, the municipal coffers needed replenishing.

Shaggy old Ganpat Ram, who was bent double and couldn't straighten up, didn't like it at all and told me so. 'If I had known this was going to happen,' he mumbled, 'I would have chosen some other line of work.'

Ganpat Ram was an aristocrat among beggars. I had heard that he had once been a man of property with several houses and a European wife. When his wife packed up and returned to Europe, together with all their savings, Ganpat had a nervous breakdown from which he never recovered. His health became steadily worse until he had to hobble about with a stick. He never made a direct request for money but greeted you politely, commented on the weather or the price of things, and stood significantly beside you.

I suspected his story to be half true because whenever he approached a well-dressed person, he used impeccable English. He had a white beard and twinkling eyes and was not the sort of beggar who invokes the names of the gods and calls on the mercy of the passer-by. Ganpat would rely more on a good joke. Some said he was a spy or a policeman in disguise, but so devoted to his work that he would probably remain a beggar for five more years.

'Look, Ganpat,' I said one day, 'I've heard a lot of stories about you and I don't know which is true. How did you get your crooked back?'

'That's a very long story,' he said, flattered by my interest in him. 'And I don't know if you will believe it. Besides, it is not to everyone that I would speak freely.'

He had served his purpose of whetting my appetite. I said, 'I'll give you four annas if you tell me your story. How about that?'

He stroked his beard, considering my offer. 'All right,' he said, squatting down on his haunches in the sunshine, while I pulled myself up on a low wall. 'But it happened more than twenty years ago and you cannot expect me to remember very clearly.'

In those days (said Ganpat) I was quite a young man and had just been married. I owned several acres of land and, though we were not rich, we were not very poor. When I took my produce to the market, five miles away, I harnessed the bullocks and drove down the dusty village road. I would return home at night.

Every night, I passed a peepal tree, and it was said this tree was haunted. I had never met the ghost and did not believe in him but his name, I was told, was Bippin, and long ago he had been hanged from the peepal tree by a band of dacoits. Ever since, his ghost had lived in the tree, and was in the habit of pouncing upon any person who resembled a dacoit and beating him severely. I suppose I must have looked dishonest, for one night Bippin decided to pounce on me. He leapt out of the tree and stood in the middle of the road, blocking the way.

'You, there!' he shouted. 'Get off your cart. I am going to kill you!'

I was, of course, taken aback, but saw no reason why I should obey.

'I have no intention of being killed,' I said. 'Get on the cart yourself!'

'Spoken like a man!' cried Bippin, and he jumped up on the cart beside me. 'But tell me one good reason why I should not kill you?'

'I am not a dacoit,' I replied.

'But you look like one. That is the same thing.'

'You would be sorry for it later if you killed me. I am a poor man with a wife to support.'

'You have no reason for being poor,' said Bippin angrily.

'Well, make me rich if you can.'

'So you think I don't have the power to make you rich? Do you defy me to make you rich?'

'Yes,' I said. 'I defy you to make me rich.'

'Then drive on!' cried Bippin. 'I am coming home with you.' I drove the bullock-cart into the village with Bippin sitting beside me.

'I have so arranged it,' he said, 'that no one but you will be able to see me. And another thing. I must sleep beside you, every night and no one must know of it. If you tell anyone about me, I'll kill you immediately!'

'Don't worry,' I said. 'I won't tell anyone.'

'Good. I look forward to living with you. It was getting lonely in that pipal tree.'

So Bippin came to live with me, and he slept beside me every night and we got on very well together. He was as good as his word and money began to pour in from every conceivable and inconceivable source until I was in a position to buy more land, and cattle. Nobody knew of our association though of course my friends and relatives wondered where all the money was coming from. At the same time, my wife was rather upset at my refusing to sleep with her at night. I could not very well keep her in the same bed as a ghost and Bippin was most particular about sleeping beside me. At first, I had told my wife I wasn't well, that I would sleep on the veranda. Then I told her that there was someone after our cows, and I would have to keep an eye on them at night.

Ruskin Bond

Bippin and I slept in the barn.

My wife would often spy on me at night, suspecting infidelity, but she always found me lying alone with the cows. Unable to understand my strange behaviour, she mentioned it to her family. They came to me demanding an explanation.

At the same time, my own relatives were insisting that I tell them the source of my increasing income. Uncles and aunts and distant cousins all descended on me one day, wanting to know where the money was coming from.

'Do you want me to die?' I said, losing patience with them. 'If I tell you the cause of my wealth, I will surely die.'

But they laughed, taking this for a half-hearted excuse. They suspected I was trying to keep everything for myself. My wife's relatives insisted that I had found another woman. Eventually, I grew so exhausted with their demands that I blurted out the truth.

They didn't believe the truth either (who does?), but it gave them something to think and talk about and they went away for the time being.

But that night, Bippin didn't come to sleep beside me. I was all alone with the cows. And he didn't come the following night. I had been afraid he would kill me while I slept but it appeared that he had gone his way and left me to my own devices. I was certain that my good fortune had come to an end and so I went back to sleeping with my wife.

The next time I was driving back to the village from the market, Bippin leapt out of the peepal tree.

'False friend!' he cried, halting the bullocks. 'I gave you everything you wanted and still you betrayed me!'

'I'm sorry,' I said. 'You can kill me if you like.'

'No, I cannot kill you,' he said. 'We have been friends for too long. But I will punish you all the same.'

Picking up a stout stick, he struck me three times across the back, until I was bent up double.

'After that,' Ganpat concluded, 'I could never straighten up again and, for over twenty years, I have been a crooked man. My wife left me and went back to her family and I could no longer work in the fields. I left my village and wandered, from one city to another, begging for a living. That is how I came to Pipalnagar where I decided to remain. People here seem to be more generous than they are in other towns,

Ruskin Bond

perhaps because they haven't got so much.'

He looked up at me with a smile, waiting for me to produce the four annas.

'You can't expect me to believe that story,' I said. 'But it was a good invention. So here is your money.'

'No, no!' said Ganpat, backing away and affecting indignation. 'If you don't believe me, keep the money. I would not lie to you for a mere four annas!'

He permitted me to force the coin into his hand and then went hobbling away, having first wished me a pleasant afternoon.

I was almost certain he had been telling me a very tall story; but you never can tell . . . Perhaps he really had met Bippin the ghost. And it was wise to give him the four annas, just in case, after all, he was a CID man.

twenty-one

listen to the wind

March is probably the most uncomfortable month in the hills. The rain is cold, often accompanied by sleet and hail, and the wind from the north comes tearing down the mountain-passes with tremendous force. Those few people who pass the winter in the hill station remain close to their fires. If they can't afford fires they get into bed.

I found old Miss Mackenzie tucked up in bed with three hot-water bottles for company. I took the bedroom's single easy chair, and for some time Miss Mackenzie and I listened to the thunder and watched the play of lightning. The rain made a tremendous noise on the corrugated tin roof, and we had to raise our voices in order to be heard. The hills looked blurred and smudgy when seen through the rain-spattered windows. The wind battered at the doors and rushed round the cottage, determined to make an entry; it slipped down the chimney, but stuck there choking and gurgling and protesting helplessly.

'There's a ghost in your chimney and he can't get out,' I said.

'Then let him stay there,' said Miss Mackenzie.

A vivid flash of lightning lit up the opposite hill, showing me for a moment a pile of ruins which I never knew were there.

'You're looking at Burnt Hill,' said Miss Mackenzie. 'It always gets the lightning when there's a storm.'

'Possibly there are iron deposits in the rocks,' I said.

'I wouldn't know. But it's the reason why no one ever lived there for long. Almost every dwelling that was put up was struck by lightning and burnt down.'

'I thought I saw some ruins just now.'

'Nothing but rubble. When they were first settling in the hills they chose that spot. Later they moved to the site where the town now stands. Burnt Hill was left to the deer and the leopards and the monkeys—and to its ghosts, of course . . .'

'Oh, so it's haunted, too.'

'So they say. On evenings such as these. But you don't believe in ghosts, do you?'

'No. Do you?'

'No. But you'll understand why they say the hill is haunted when you hear its story. Listen.'

I listened, but at first I could hear nothing but the wind and the rain. Then Miss Mackenzie's clear voice rose above the sound of the elements, and I heard her saying:

'. . . it's really the old story of ill-starred lovers, only it's true. I'd met Robert at his parents' house some weeks before the tragedy took place. He was eighteen, tall and fresh-looking, and full of manhood. He'd been born out here, but his parents were hoping to return to England when Robert's father retired. His father was a magistrate, I think—but that hasn't any bearing on the story.

'Their plans didn't work out the way they expected. You see, Robert fell in love. Not with an English girl, mind you, but with a hill girl, the daughter of a landholder from the village behind Burnt Hill. Even today it would be unconventional. Twenty-five years ago, it was almost unheard of! Robert liked walking and he was hiking through the forest when he

Ruskin Bond

saw or rather heard her. It was said later that he fell in love with her voice. She was singing, and the song—low and sweet and strange to his ears—struck him to the heart. When he caught sight of the girl's face, he was not disappointed. She was young and beautiful. She saw him and returned his awestruck gaze with a brief, fleeting smile.

'Robert, in his impetuousness, made enquiries at the village, located the girl's father, and without much ado asked for her hand in marriage. He probably thought that a sahib would not be refused such a request. At the same time, it was really quite gallant on his part, because any other young man might simply have ravished the girl in the forest. But Robert was in love and, therefore, completely irrational in his behaviour.

'Of course the girl's father would have nothing to do with the proposal. He was a Brahmin, and he wasn't going to have the good name of his family ruined by marrying off his only daughter to a foreigner. Robert did not argue with the father; nor did he say anything to his own parents, because he knew their reaction would be one of shock and dismay. They would do everything in their power to put an end to his madness.

'But Robert continued to visit the forest—you see it there, that heavy patch of oak and pine—and he often came across the girl, for she would be gathering fodder or fuel. She did not seem to resent his attentions, and, as Robert knew something of the language, he was soon able to convey his feelings to her. The girl must at first have been rather alarmed, but the boy's sincerity broke down her reserve. After all, she was young too—young enough to fall in love with a devoted swain, without thinking too much of his background. She knew her father would never agree to a marriage—and he knew his parents would prevent anything like that happening. So they planned to run away together. Romantic, isn't it? But it did happen. Only they did *not* live happily ever after.'

'Did their parents come after them?'

'No. They had agreed to meet one night in the ruined building on Burnt Hill—the ruin you saw just now; it hasn't changed much, except that there was a bit of roof to it then. They left their homes and made their way to the hill without any difficulty. After meeting, they planned to take the little path that followed the course of a stream until it reached the plains. After that—but who knows what they had planned, what dreams of the future they had conjured up? The storm broke soon after they'd reached the ruins. They took shelter under the dripping ceiling. It was a storm just like this one—a high wind and great torrents of rain and hail, and the lightning flitting about and crashing down almost every minute. They must have been soaked, huddled together in a corner of that crumbling building, when lightning struck. No one knows at what time it happened. But next morning their charred bodies were found on the worn yellow stones of the old building.'

Miss Mackenzie stopped speaking, and I noticed that the thunder had grown distant and the rain had lessened; but the chimney was still coughing and clearing its throat.

'That's true, every word of it,' said Miss Mackenzie. 'But as to Burnt Hill being haunted, that's another matter. I've no experience of ghosts.'

'Anyway, you need a fire to keep them out of the chimney,' I said, getting up to go. I had my raincoat and umbrella, and my own cottage was not far away.

Next morning, when I took the steep path up to Burnt Hill, the sky was clear, and though there was still a stiff wind, it was no longer menacing. An hour's climb brought me to the old ruin—now nothing but a heap of stones, as Miss Mackenzie had said. Part of a wall was left, and the corner of a fireplace. Grass and weeds had grown up through the floor, and primroses and wild saxifrage flowered amongst the rubble.

Where had they sheltered, I wondered, as the wind tore at them and fire fell from the sky.

I touched the cold stones, half expecting to find in them some traces of the warmth of human contact. I listened, waiting for some ancient echo, some returning wave of sound, that would bring me nearer to the spirits of the dead lovers; but there was only the wind coughing in the lovely pines.

I thought I heard voices in the wind; and perhaps I did. For isn't the wind the voice of the undying dead?

Ruskin Bond

ghosts of the savoy

Whose ghost was it that Ram Singh (the Savoy bartender) saw last night? A figure in a long black cloak, who stood for a few moments in the hotel's dimly lit vestibule, and then moved into the shadows of the old lounge. Ram Singh followed the figure, but there was no one in the lounge and no door or window through which the man (if it was a man) had made his exit.

Ram Singh doesn't tipple; or so he says. Nor is he the imaginative type.

'Have you seen this person—this ghost— before?' I asked him.

'Yes, once. Last winter, when I was passing the ballroom, I heard someone playing the piano. The ballroom door was locked, and I couldn't get in nor could anyone else. I stood on a ledge and looked through one of the windows, and there was this person—a hooded figure, I could not see the face—sitting on the piano stool. I could hear the music playing, and I tapped on the window. The figure turned towards me, but the hood was empty, there was nothing there to see! I ran to my room and bolted the door. We should sell that piano, sir. There's no one here to play it apart from the ghost.'

Almost any story about this old hotel in Mussoorie has a touch of the improbable about it, even when supported by facts. A previous owner, Mr McClintock, had a false nose—according to Nandu, who never saw it. So I checked with old Negi, who first came to work in the hotel as a room boy back in 1932 (a couple of years before I was born) and who, almost seventy years and two wives later, looks after the front office. Negi tells me it's quite true.

'I used to take McClintock sahib his cup of cocoa last thing at night. After leaving his room I'd dash around to one of the windows and watch him until he went to bed. The last thing he did, before putting the light out, was to remove his false nose and place it on the

Ruskin Bond

bedside table. He never slept with it on. I suppose it bothered him whenever he turned over or slept on his face. First thing in the morning, before having his cup of tea, he'd put it on again. A great man, McClintock sahib.'

'But how did he lose his nose in the first place?' I asked.

'Wife bit it off,' said Nandu.

'No, sir,' said Negi, whose reputation for telling the truth is proverbial. 'It was shot away by a German bullet during World War I. He got the Victoria Cross as compensation.'

'And when he died, was he wearing his nose?' I asked.

'No, sir,' said old Negi, continuing his tale with some relish. 'One morning when I took the sahib his cup of tea, I found him stone dead, without his nose! It was lying on the bedside table. I suppose I should have left it there, but McClintock sahib was a good man, I could not bear to have the whole world knowing about his false nose. So I stuck it back on his face and then went and informed the manager. A natural death, just a sudden heart attack. But I made sure that he went into his coffin with his nose attached!'

We all agreed that Negi was a good man to have around, especially in a crisis.

McClintock's ghost is supposed to haunt the corridors of the hotel, but I have yet to encounter it. Will the ghost be wearing its nose? Old Negi thinks not (the false nose being man-made), but then he hasn't seen the ghost at close quarters, only receding into the distance between the two giant deodars on the edge of the beer garden.

A lot of people who enter the Writers' Bar look pretty far gone, and sometimes I have difficulty distinguishing the living from the dead. But the real ghosts are those who manage to slip away without paying for their drinks.

Ruskin Bond

the man who
was kipling

I was sitting on a bench in the Indian section of the Victoria and Albert Museum, when a tall, stooping, elderly gentleman sat down beside me. I gave him a quick glance, noting his swarthy features, heavy moustache, and horn-rimmed spectacles. There was something familiar and disturbing about his face and I couldn't resist looking at him again.

I noticed that he was smiling at me.

'Do you recognize me?' he asked in a soft pleasant voice.

'Well, you do seem familiar,' I said. 'Haven't we met somewhere?'

'Perhaps. But if I seem familiar to you, that is at least something. The trouble these days is that people don't know me anymore—I'm a familiar, that's all. Just a name standing for a lot of outmoded ideas.'

A little perplexed, I asked, 'What is it you do?'

'I wrote books once. Poems and tales . . . Tell me, whose books do you read?'

'Oh, Maugham, Priestley, Thurber. And among the older lot, Bennett and Wells . . .' I hesitated, groping for an important name, and I noticed a shadow, a sad shadow, pass across my companion's face.

'Oh yes, and Kipling,' I said. 'I read a lot of Kipling.'

His face brightened up at once and the eyes behind the thick-lensed spectacles suddenly came to life.

'I'm Kipling,' he said.

I stared at him in astonishment. And then, realizing that he might perhaps be dangerous, I smiled feebly and said, 'Oh yes?'

'You probably don't believe me. I'm dead, of course.'

'So I thought.'

'And you don't believe in ghosts?'

'Not as a rule.'

'But you'd have no objection to talking to one if he came along?'

'I'd have no objection. But how do I know you're Kipling? How do I know you're not an impostor?'

'Listen, then:

When my heavens were turned to blood,
When the dark had filled my day,
Furthest, but most faithful, stood
That lone star I cast away.
I had loved myself, and I
Have not lived and dare not die.

'Once,' he said, gripping me by the arm and looking me straight in the eye. 'Once in life I watched a star but I whistled her to go.'

'Your star hasn't fallen yet,' I said, suddenly moved, suddenly quite certain that I sat beside Kipling. 'One day, when there is a new spirit of adventure abroad, we will discover you again.'

'Why have they heaped scorn on me for so long?'

'You were too militant, I suppose—too much of an Empire man. You were too patriotic for your own good.'

He looked a little hurt. 'I was never very political,' he said. 'I wrote over 600 poems. And you could only call a dozen of them political. I have been abused for harping on the theme of the White Man's burden but my only aim was to show off the Empire to my audience—and I believed the Empire was a fine and noble thing. Is it wrong to believe in something? I never went deeply into political issues, that's true. You must remember, my seven years in India were very youthful years. I was in my twenties, a little immature if you like, and my interest in India was a boy's interest. Action appealed to me more than anything else. You must understand that.'

'No one has described action more vividly, or India so well. I feel at one with Kim wherever he goes along the Grand Trunk Road, in the temples at Banaras, amongst the Saharanpur fruit gardens, on the snow-covered Himalayas. *Kim* has colour and movement and poetry.'

He sighed and a wistful look came into his eyes.

'I'm prejudiced, of course,' I continued. 'I've spent most of my life in India—not *your* India, but an India that does still have much of the colour and atmosphere that you captured. You know, Mr Kipling, you can still sit in a third-class railway carriage and meet the most wonderful assortment of people. In any village you will still find the same courtesy, dignity and courage that the Lama and Kim found on their travels.'

Ruskin Bond

'And the Grand Trunk Road? Is it still a long winding procession of humanity?'

'Well, not exactly,' I said a little ruefully. 'It's just a procession of motor vehicles now. The poor Lama would be run down by a truck if he became too dreamy on the Grand Trunk Road. Times *have* changed. There are no more Mrs Hawksbees in Simla, for instance.'

There was a faraway look in Kipling's eyes. Perhaps he was imagining himself a boy again. Perhaps he could see the hills or the red dust of Rajputana. Perhaps he was having a private conversation with Privates Mulvaney and Ortheris, or perhaps he was out hunting with the Seonce wolf-pack. The sound of London's traffic came to us through the glass doors but we heard only the creaking of bullock-cart wheels and the distant music of a flute.

He was talking to himself, repeating a passage from one of his stories. 'And the last puff of the daywind brought from the unseen villages the scent of damp wood-smoke, hot cakes, dripping undergrowth, and rotting pine-cones. That is the true smell of the Himalayas and if once it creeps into the blood of a man, that man will at the last, forgetting all else, return to the hills to die.'

A mist seemed to have risen between us—

or had it come in from the streets?—and when it cleared, Kipling had gone away.

I asked the gatekeeper if he had seen a tall man with a slight stoop, wearing spectacles.

'Nope,' said the gatekeeper. 'Nobody's been by for the last ten minutes.'

'Did someone like that come into the gallery a little while ago?'

'No one that I recall. What did you say the bloke's name was?'

'Kipling,' I said.

'Don't know him.'

'Didn't you ever read *The Jungle Books*?'

'Sounds familiar. Tarzan stuff, wasn't it?'

I left the museum and wandered about the streets for a long time but I couldn't find Kipling anywhere. Was it the boom of London's traffic that I heard or the boom of the Sutlej river racing through the valleys?

Ruskin Bond

twenty-four

the daffodil case

It was a foggy day in March that found me idling along Baker Street, with my hands in my raincoat pockets, a threadbare scarf wound round my neck, and two pairs of socks on my feet. The BBC had commissioned me to give a talk on village life in northern India, and, ambling along Baker Street in the fog, thinking about the talk, I realized that I didn't really know very much about village life in India or anywhere else.

True, I could recall the smell of cowdung smoke and the scent of jasmine and the flood waters lapping at the walls of mud houses, but I didn't know much about village electorates or crop rotation or sugarcane prices. I was on the point of turning back and making my way to

India House to get a few facts and figures when I realized I wasn't on Baker Street any more.

Wrapped in thought, I had wandered into Regent's Park. And now I wasn't sure of the way out.

A tall gentleman wearing a long grey cloak was stooping over a flower-bed. Going up to him, I asked, 'Excuse me, sir—can you tell me how I get out of here?'

'How did you get in?' he asked in an impatient tone, and when he turned and faced me, I received quite a shock. He wore a peaked hunting-cap, and in one hand he held a large magnifying glass. A long curved pipe hung from his sensuous lips. He possessed a strong, steely jaw and his eyes had a fierce expression—they were bright with the intoxication of some drug.

'Good heavens!' I exclaimed. 'You're Sherlock Holmes!'

'And you, sir,' he replied, with a flourish of his cloak, 'are just out of India, unemployed, and due to give a lecture on the radio.'

'How did you know all that?' I stammered. 'You've never seen me before. I suppose you know my name, too?'

'Elementary, my dear Bond. The BBC

notepaper in your hand, on which you have been scribbling, reveals your intentions. You are unsure of yourself, so you are not a TV personality. But you have a considered and considerate tone of voice. Definitely radio. Your name is on the envelope which you are holding upside down. It's Bond, but you're definitely not James— you're not the type! You have to be unemployed, otherwise what would you be doing in the Park when the rest of mankind is hard at work in office, field, or factory?'

'And how do you know I'm from India?' I asked, a little resentfully.

'Your accent betrays you,' said Holmes with a knowing smile.

I was about to turn away and leave him when he laid a restraining hand on my shoulder.

'Stay a moment,' he said. 'Perhaps you can be of assistance. I'm surprised at Watson. He promised to be here fifteen minutes ago but his wife must have kept him at home. Never marry, Bond. Women sap the intellect.'

'In what way can I help you?' I asked, feeling flattered now that the great man had condescended to take me into his confidence.

'Take a look at this,' said Holmes, going down on his knees near a flower-bed. 'Do you notice anything unusual?'

The Daffodil Case   {169}

'Someone's been pulling out daffodils,' I said.

'Excellent, Bond! Your power of observation is as good as Watson's. Now tell me, what else do you see?'

'The ground is a little trampled, that's all.'

'By what?'

'A human foot. In high heels. And . . . a dog has been here too, it's been helping to dig up the bulbs!'

'You astonish me, Bond. You are quicker than I thought you'd be. Now shall I explain what this is all about? You see, for the past week someone has been stealing daffodils from the park, and the authorities have now asked me to deal with the matter. I think we shall catch our culprit today.'

I was rather disappointed. 'It isn't dangerous work, then?'

'Ah, my dear Bond, the days are past when Ruritanian princes lost their diamonds and Maharanis their rubies. There are no longer any Ruritanian princes and Maharanis cannot afford rubies—unless they've gone into the fast-food business. The more successful criminals now work on the stock exchange, and the East End has been cleaned up. Dr Fu Manchu has a country house in Dorset. And those cretins at

Scotland Yard don't even believe in my existence!'

'I'm sorry to hear that,' I said. 'But who do you think is stealing the daffodils?'

'Obviously it's someone who owns a dog. Someone who takes a dog out regularly for a morning walk. That points to a woman. A woman in London is likely to keep a small dog—and, judging from the animal's footprints, it was a little Pekinese or a very young Pomeranian. If you observe the damp patch on that lamp-post, you will realize that it could not have been very tall. So what I propose, Bond, is that we conceal ourselves behind this herbaceous border and wait for the culprit to return to the scene of the crime. She is sure to come again this morning. She has been stealing daffodils for the past week. And stealing daffodils, like smoking opium, soon becomes a habit.'

Holmes and I concealed ourselves behind the hedge and settled down to a long wait. After half an hour, our patience was rewarded. An elderly but upright woman in a smart green hat, resembling Margaret Thatcher, came walking towards us across the grass, followed by a small white Pom on a lead. Holmes had been right! More than ever did I admire his brilliance. We waited until the woman began pulling daffodil bulbs out of the loose soil, then Holmes leapt from the bushes.

'Ah, we have you, madam!' he cried springing upon her so swiftly that she shrieked and dropped the daffodils. I bent over to gather the evidence, but my efforts were rewarded by a nip on the posterior from the outraged Pomeranian.

Holmes was restraining the woman simply by peering at her heaving bosom through his magnifying glass. I don't know what frightened her more—being caught, or being confronted by that grim-visaged countenance, with its pipe, cloak and hunting-cap.

'Now, madam,' he said firmly, 'why were you stealing her Majesty's daffodils?'

She had begun to weep—always a woman's best defence—and I thought Holmes would soften. He always did when confronted by weeping women. And this wasn't Mrs Thatcher; she would have gone on the offensive.

'I would be obliged, Bond, if you would call the park attendant,' he said.

I hurried off to a distant greenhouse and after a brief search found a gardener. 'Stealing daffodils, is she?' he said, running up at the double, a wicked-looking rake in one hand.

But when he got to the daffodil-bed, we couldn't find the thief anywhere. Nor was Holmes to be seen. Apparently they'd gone off together, leaving me in the lurch. I was overcome by doubt and embarrassment. But then I looked at the ground and saw daffodil bulbs scattered about on the grass.

'Holmes must have taken her to the police,' I said.

'Holmes,' repeated the gardener. 'And who's Holmes?'

'Sherlock Holmes, of course. The celebrated detective. Haven't you heard of him?'

The gardener gave me a suspicious look.

'Sherlock Holmes, eh? And you'll be Dr Watson, I presume?'

'Well, no,' I said apologetically. 'The name is Bond.'

That was enough for the gardener. He'd seen madmen in the park before. He turned and disappeared in the direction of the greenhouse.

Eventually I found my way out of the park, feeling that Holmes had let me down a little. Then, just as I was crossing Baker Street, I thought I saw him on the opposite curb. He was alone, looking up at a lighted room, and his arm was raised as though he was waving to someone. I thought I heard him shout 'Watson!', but I couldn't be sure. I started to cross the road, but a big red bus came out of the fog in front of me and I had to wait for it to pass. When the road was clear, I dashed across. By that time, Mr Holmes had gone, and the rooms above were dark.

twenty-five

picnic at fox-burn

In spite of the frenetic building activity in most hill stations, there are still a few ruins to be found on the outskirts—neglected old bungalows that have fallen or been pulled down, and which now provide shelter for bats, owls, stray goats, itinerant sadhus, and sometimes the restless spirits of those who once dwelt in them.

One such ruin is Fox-Burn, but I won't tell you exactly where it can be found, because I visit the place for purposes of meditation (or just plain contemplation) and I would hate to arrive there one morning to find about fifty people picnicking on the grass.

And yet it did witness a picnic of sorts the other day, when the children accompanied me to the ruin. They had heard it was haunted, and they wanted to see the ghost.

Rakesh is twelve, Mukesh is six, and Dolly is four, and they are not afraid of ghosts.

I should mention here that before Fox-Burn became a ruin, back in the 1940s, it was owned by an elderly English woman, Mrs Williams, who ran it as a boarding house for several years. In the end, poor health forced her to give up this work, and during her last years, she lived alone in the huge house, with just a chowkidar to help. Her children, who had grown up on the property, had long since settled in faraway lands.

When Mrs Williams died, the chowkidar stayed on for some time until the property was disposed of; but he left as soon as he could. Late at night there would be a loud rapping on his door, and he would hear the old lady calling out, 'Shamsher Singh, open the door! Open the door, I say, and let me in!'

Needless to say, Shamsher Singh kept the door firmly closed. He returned to his village at the first opportunity. The hill station was going through a slump at the time, and the new owners pulled the house down and sold the roof and beams as scrap.

'What does Fox-Burn mean?' asked Rakesh,

as we climbed the neglected, overgrown path to the ruin.

'Well, Burn is a Scottish word meaning stream or spring. Perhaps there was a spring here, once. If so, it dried up long ago.'

'And did a fox live here?'

'Maybe a fox came to drink at the spring. There are still foxes living on the mountain. Sometimes you can see them dancing in the moonlight.'

Passing through a gap in a wall, we came upon the ruins of the house. In the bright light of a summer morning it did not look in the least spooky or depressing. A line of Doric pillars were all that remained of what must have been an elegant porch and veranda. Beyond them, through the deodars, we could see the distant snows. It must have been a lovely spot in which to spend the better part of one's life. No wonder Mrs Williams wanted to come back.

The children were soon scampering about on the grass, while I sought shelter beneath a huge chestnut tree.

There is no tree so friendly as the chestnut, specially in summer when it is in full leaf.

Mukesh discovered an empty water tank and Rakesh suggested that it had once fed the burn that no longer existed. Dolly busied herself making nosegays with the daisies that grew wild in the grass.

Rakesh looked up suddenly. He pointed to a path on the other side of the ruin, and exclaimed: 'Look, what's that? Is it Mrs Williams?'

'A ghost!' said Mukesh excitedly.

But it turned out to be the local washerwoman, a large white bundle on her head, taking a short cut across the property.

A more peaceful place could hardly be imagined, until a large black dog, a spaniel of sorts, arrived on the scene. He wanted someone to play with—indeed, he insisted on playing— and ran circles round us until we threw sticks for him to fetch and gave him half our sandwiches.

'Whose dog is it?' asked Rakesh.

'I've no idea.'

'Did Mrs Williams keep a black dog?'

'Is it a *ghost* dog?' asked Mukesh.

'It looks real to me,' I said.

'And it's eaten all my biscuits,' said Dolly.

'Don't ghosts have to eat?' asked Mukesh.

'I don't know. We'll have to ask one.'

'It can't be any fun being a ghost if you can't eat,' declared Mukesh.

The black dog left us as suddenly as he had appeared, and as there was no sign of an owner, I began to wonder if he had not, after all, been an apparition.

A cloud came over the sun, the air grew chilly.

'Let's go home,' said Mukesh.

'I'm hungry,' said Rakesh.

'Come along, Dolly,' I called.

But Dolly couldn't be seen.

We called out to her, and looked behind trees and pillars, certain that she was hiding from us. Almost five minutes passed in searching for her, and a sick feeling of apprehension was coming over me, when Dolly emerged from the ruins and ran towards us.

'Where have you been?' we demanded, almost with one voice.

'I was playing—in there—in the old house. Hide-and-seek.'

'On your own?'

'No, there were two children. A boy and a girl. They were playing too.'

'I haven't seen any children,' I said.

'They've gone now.'

'Well, it's time we went too.'

We set off down the winding path, with Rakesh leading the way, and then we had to wait because Dolly had stopped and was waving to someone.

'Who are you waving to, Dolly?'

'To the children.'

'Where are they?'

'Under the chestnut tree.'

'I can't see them. Can you see them, Rakesh? Can you, Mukesh?'

Rakesh and Mukesh said they couldn't see any children. But Dolly was still waving.

'Goodbye,' she called. 'Goodbye!'

Were there voices on the wind? Faint voices calling goodbye? Could Dolly see something we couldn't see?

'We can't see anyone,' I said.

'No,' said Dolly. 'But they can see me!'

Then she left off her game and joined us, and we ran home laughing. Mrs Williams may not have revisited her old house that day but perhaps her children had been there, playing under the chestnut tree they had known so long ago.

twenty-six

something in the water

I discovered the pool near Rajpur on a hot summer's day some fifteen years ago. It was shaded by close-growing sal trees, and looked cool and inviting. I took off my clothes and dived in.

The water was colder than I had expected. It was an icy glacial cold. The sun never touched it for long, I supposed. Striking out vigorously, I swam to the other end of the pool and pulled myself up on the rocks, shivering.

But I wanted to swim some more. So I dived in again and did a gentle breaststroke towards the middle of the pool. Something slid between my legs. Something slimy, pulpy. I could see no one, hear nothing. I swam away, but the slippery floating thing followed me. I did not like it. Something curled around my leg. Not an underwater plant. Something that sucked at my foot. A long tongue licked my calf. I struck out wildly, thrust myself away from whatever it was that sought my company. Something lonely, lurking in the shadows. Kicking up spray, I swam like a frightened porpoise fleeing from some terror of the deep.

Safely out of the water, I found a warm sunny rock and stood there looking down at the water.

Nothing stirred. The surface of the pool was now calm and undisturbed. Just a few fallen leaves floating around. Not a frog, not a fish, not a waterbird in sight. And that in itself seemed strange. For you would have expected some sort of pond life to have been in evidence.

But something lived in the pool, of that I was sure. Something very cold-blooded, colder and wetter than the water. Could it have been a corpse trapped in the weeds? I did not want to know; so I dressed and hurried away.

A few days later I left for Delhi, where I went to work in an ad agency, telling people how to beat the summer heat by drinking fizzy drinks that made you more thirsty. The pool in the forest was forgotten.

It was ten years before I visited Rajpur

again. Leaving the small hotel where I was staying, I found myself walking through the same old sal forest, drawn almost irresistibly towards the pool where I had not been able to finish my swim. I was not over-eager to swim there again, but I was curious to know if the pool still existed.

Well, it was there all right, although the surroundings had changed and a number of new houses and other buildings had come up where formerly there had only been wilderness. And there was a fair amount of activity in the vicinity of the pool.

A number of labourers were busy with buckets and rubber pipes, draining water from the pool. They had also dammed off and diverted the little stream that fed it.

Overseeing this operation was a well-dressed man in a white safari suit. I thought at first that he was an honorary forest warden, but it turned out that he was the owner of a new school that had been set up nearby.

'Do you live in Rajpur?' he asked.

'I used to . . . Once upon a time . . . Why are you emptying the pool?'

'It's become a hazard,' he said. 'Two of my boys were drowned here recently. Both senior students. Of course they weren't supposed to be swimming here without permission, the pool is off-limits. But you know what boys are like. Make a rule and they feel duty-bound to break it.'

He told me his name was Kapoor, and led me back to his house, a newly-built bungalow with a wide cool veranda. His servant brought us glasses of cold sherbet. We sat in cane chairs overlooking the pool and the forest. Across a clearing, a gravelled road led to the school buildings, newly whitewashed and glistening in the sun.

'Were the boys there at the same time?' I asked.

'Yes, they were friends. And they must have been attacked by absolute fiends. Limbs twisted and broken, faces disfigured. But death was due to drowning—that was the verdict of the medical examiner.'

We gazed down at the shallows of the pool, where a couple of men were still at work, the others having gone for their midday meal.

'Perhaps it would be better to leave the place alone,' I said. 'Put a barbed wire fence around it. Keep your boys away. Thousands of years ago, this valley was an inland sea. A few small pools and streams are all that is left of it.'

Ruskin Bond

'I want to fill it in and build something there. An open-air theatre, maybe. We can always create an artificial pond somewhere else.'

Presently only one man remained at the pool, knee-deep in muddy churned-up water. And Mr Kapoor and I both saw what happened next.

Something rose out of the bottom of the pool. It looked like a giant snail, but its head was part-human, its body and limbs part-squid or octopus. An enormous succubi. It stood taller than the man in the pool. A creature soft and slimy, a survivor from our primaeval past.

With a great sucking motion, it enveloped the man completely so that only his arms and legs could be seen thrashing about wildly and futilely. The succubi dragged him down under the water.

Kapoor and I left the veranda and ran to the edge of the pool. Bubbles rose from the green scum near the surface. All was still and silent. And then, like bubblegum issuing from the mouth of a child, the mangled body of the man shot out of the water and came spinning towards us.

Dead and drowned and sucked dry of its fluids.

Naturally no more work was done at the pool. The story was put out that the labourer had slipped and fallen to his death on the rocks. Kapoor swore me to secrecy. His school would have to close down if there were too many strange drownings and accidents in its vicinity. But he walled the place off from his property and made it practically inaccessible. The dense undergrowth of the sal forest now hides the approach.

The monsoon rains came and the pool filled up again.

I can tell you how to get there if you'd like to see it. But I wouldn't advise you to go for a swim.

twenty-seven

the family ghost

'Now tell us a ghost story,' I told Bibiji, my landlady, one evening, as she made herself comfortable on the old couch in the veranda. 'There must have been at least one ghost in your village.'

'Oh, there were many,' said Bibiji, who never tired of telling weird tales. 'Wicked *churel*s and mischievous *pret*s. And there was a *munjia* who ran away.'

'What is a *munjia*?' I asked.

'A *munjia* is the ghost of a brahmin youth who had committed suicide on the eve of his marriage. Our village *munjia* had taken up residence in an old peepal tree.'

'I wonder why ghosts always live in peepal trees!' I said.

'I'll tell you about that another time,' said Bibiji. 'But listen to the story about the *munjia* . . .'

Near the village peepal tree (according to Bibiji) there lived a family of brahmins who were under the special protection of this *munjia*. The ghost had attached himself to this particular family (they were related to the girl to whom he had once been betrothed) and showed his fondness for them by throwing stones, bones, night soil and rubbish at them, making hideous noises, and terrifying them whenever he found an opportunity. Under his patronage, the family soon dwindled away. One by one they died, the only survivor being an idiot boy, whom the ghost did not bother, because he thought it beneath his dignity to do so.

But, in a village, birth, marriage and death must come to all, and so it was not long before the neighbours began to make plans for the marriage of the idiot.

After a meeting of the village elders, they agreed, first, that the idiot should be married; and second, that he should be married to a shrew of a girl who had reached the age of sixteen without finding a suitor.

The shrew and the idiot were soon married off, and then left to manage for themselves.

The poor idiot had no means of earning a living and had to resort to begging. Previously, he had barely been able to support himself, and now his wife was an additional burden. The first thing she did when she entered his house was to give him a box on the ear and send him out to bring something home for their dinner.

The poor fellow went from door to door, but nobody gave him anything, because the same people who had arranged his marriage were annoyed that he had not given them a wedding feast. When, in the evening, he returned home empty-handed, his wife cried out, 'Are you back, you lazy idiot? Where have you been so long, and what have you brought for me?'

When she found he hadn't even a paisa, she flew into a rage and, tearing off his turban, threw it into the peepal tree. Then, taking up her broom, she thrashed her husband until he fled from the house, howling with pain.

But the shrew's anger had not yet diminished. Seeing her husband's turban in the peepal tree, she began to beat the tree trunk, accompanying her blows with strong abuses. The ghost who lived in the tree was sensitive to her blows and, alarmed that her language might have the effect of finishing him off altogether, he took to his invisible heels, and left the tree on which he had lived for many years.

Riding on a whirlwind, the ghost soon caught up with the idiot who was still running down the road leading away from the village.

'Not so fast, brother!' cried the ghost. 'Desert your wife, certainly, but not your old family ghost! The shrew has driven me out of my peepal tree. Truly, a ghost is no match for a woman with a vile tongue! From now on we are brothers and must seek our fortunes together. But first promise me that you will not return to your wife.'

The idiot made this promise very willingly, and together they continued their journey until they reached a large city.

Before entering the city, the ghost said, 'Now listen, brother, and if you follow my advice, your fortune is made. In this city there are two very beautiful girls, one is the daughter of a Raja, and the other the daughter of a rich moneylender. I will go and possess the daughter of the Raja and her father will try every sort of remedy without effect. Meanwhile you must walk daily through the streets in the robes of a sadhu, and when the Raja comes and asks you to cure his daughter, make any terms that you think suitable. As soon as I see you, I shall leave the girl. Then I shall go and possess the daughter of the moneylender. But do not go anywhere near her, because I am in love with the girl and do not intend giving her up. If you come near her, I shall break your neck.'

The ghost went off on his whirlwind, and the idiot entered the city on his own, and found a bed in the local rest house for pilgrims.

The next day the city was agog with the news that the Raja's daughter was dangerously ill. Physicians—*hakims* and *vaids*—came and went, and all pronounced the girl incurable. The Raja was distracted with grief, and offered half his fortune to anyone who would cure his beautiful and only child. The idiot, having smeared himself with dust and ashes, began walking the streets, occasionally crying out: '*Bhum, bhum, bho! Bom Bhola Nath!*'

The people were struck by his appearance, and taking him for a wise and holy man, reported him to the Raja. The latter immediately entered the city and, prostrating himself before the idiot, begged him to cure his daughter. After a show of modesty and reluctance, the idiot was persuaded to accompany the Raja back to the palace, and the girl was brought before him.

Her hair was dishevelled, her teeth were chattering, and her eyes almost starting from their sockets. She howled and cursed and tore at her clothes. When the idiot confronted her, he recited certain meaningless spells; and the ghost, recognizing him, cried out: 'I go, I go! *Bhum, bhum, bho!*'

'Give me a sign that you have gone,' demanded the idiot.

'As soon as I leave the girl,' said the ghost, 'you will see that mango tree uprooted. That is the sign I'll give.'

A few minutes later, the mango tree came crashing down. The girl recovered from her fit, and seemed unaware of what had happened to her. The news spread through the city, and the idiot became an object of respect and wonder. The Raja kept his word and gave him half his fortune; and so began a period of happiness and prosperity for the idiot.

A few weeks later, the ghost took possession of the moneylender's daughter, with whom he was deeply in love. Seeing his daughter go out of her right senses, the moneylender sent for the highly esteemed idiot and offered him a great sum of money if he would cure his daughter. But remembering the ghost's warning, the idiot refused to go. The moneylender was enraged and sent his henchmen to bring the idiot to him by force; and the idiot, having no means of resisting, was dragged along to the rich man's house.

As soon as the ghost saw his old companion he cried out in a rage: 'Idiot, why have you broken our agreement and come here? Now I will have to break your neck!'

But the idiot, whose reputation for wisdom had actually served to make him wiser, said, 'Brother ghost, I have not come to trouble you, but to tell you a terrible piece of news. Old friend and protector, we must leave this city soon. You see, SHE has come here—my dreaded wife, the shrew!—to torment us both, and to drag us back to the village. She is on the road to this house and will be here in a few minutes!'

When the ghost heard this, he cried out: 'Oh no, oh no! If she has come, then we must go! *Bhum bho, bhum bho*, we go, we go!'

And breaking down the walls and doors of the house, the ghost gathered himself up into a little whirlwind and went scurrying out of the city, to look for a vacant peepal tree.

The moneylender, delighted that his daughter had been freed of the evil influence, embraced the idiot and showered presents on him. And in due course, concluded Bibiji, the idiot married the moneylender's beautiful daughter, inherited his father-in-law's wealth and became the richest and most successful moneylender in the city.

twenty-eight

night of the millennium

Jackals howled dismally, foraging for bones and offal down in the *khud* below the butcher's shop. Pasand was unperturbed by the sound. A robust young computer whiz-kid and patriotic multinational, he prided himself on being above and beyond all superstitious fears of the unknown. In his lexicon, the unknown was just something that was waiting to be discovered. Hence this walk past the old cemetery late at night.

Midnight would see the new millennium in. The year 2000 beckoned, full of bright prospects for well-heeled young men like Pasand. True, there were millions—soon to be over a billion—sweating it out in the heat and dust of the plains below, scraping together a meagre living for themselves and their sprawling families. Not for them the advantages of a public school education, three cars in the garage, and a bank account in Bermuda. Ah well, mused Pasand, not everyone could have the brains and good luck, as well as inherited family wealth of course, that had made life so pleasant and promising for him. This was going to be the century in which the smart-asses would get to the top and all other varieties of asses would sink to the bottom. It was important to have a ruling elite, according to his philosophy; only then could slaves prosper!

He looked at his watch. It was just past midnight. He had eaten well, and he was enjoying his little walk along the lonely winding road which took him past the houses of the rich and famous, the Lals, the Banerjees, the Kapoors, the Ramchandanis—he was as good as any of them! Better, in fact. He was approaching his own personal Everest, while they had reached theirs and were on the downward slope, or so he presumed.

Here was the cemetery with its broken old tombstones, some of them dating from a hundred and fifty years ago: pathetic reminders of a once-powerful empire, now reduced to dust and crumbling monuments. Here lay colonels and magistrates, merchants and memsahibs, and many small children; fragile lives which had been snuffed out in more turbulent times. To Pasand, they were losers, all of them. He had nothing but contempt for those who hadn't been able to hang on to their power and glory. No lost empires for him!

The road here was very dark, for the trees grew thick on the northern slopes. Pasand felt a twinge of nervousness, but he was reassured by the feel of the cellphone in his pocket—he could always summon his driver or his armed bodyguard to come and pick him up.

The moon had risen over Nag Tibba, and the graves stood out in serried rows, as though forming a guard of honour for this modern knight in T-shirt and designer jeans. Through the deodars he saw a faint light on the perimeter of the cemetery. Here, he had learnt from one of his *chamcha*s, lived a widow with a brood of small children. Although in poor health, she was still young and comely, and known to be lavish with her favours to those who were generous with their purses; for she needed the money for her hungry family.

She was also a little mad, they said, and preferred to sleep in one of the old domed tombs rather than in the quarters provided for her late husband, who had been the caretaker.

This did not bother Pasand. He was in search of sensual pleasure, not romance. And right now he felt an urgent need to exert his dominance over someone, preferably a woman, for he had to prove his manhood in some way. So far, most young women had shied away from his vainglorious and clumsy approach.

This woman wasn't young. She was in her late thirties, and poverty, malnutrition and ill-use had made her look much older. But there were vestiges of beauty in her smouldering eyes and sinewy limbs. Her gypsy blood must have had something to do with it. Her teeth gleamed in the darkness as she smiled at Pasand and invited him into her boudoir—the spacious tomb that she favoured most.

Pasand had no time for tender love-play. Clumsily he clawed at her breasts but found they were not much larger than his own. He tore at her already tattered clothes, pressed his mouth hungrily to her dry lips. She made no attempt to resist. He had his way. Then, while he lay supine across the cold damp slab of a grave that covered the remains of some long-dead warrior, she leaned over him and bit him on the cheek and neck.

He cried out in pain and astonishment, and tried to sit up. But a number of hands, small but strong, thrust him back against the tombstone. Small mouths, sharp teeth, pressed against his flesh. Muddy fingers tore at his clothes. Those young teeth bit—and bit again. His screams mingled with the cries of the jackals.

'Patience, my children, patience,' crooned the woman. 'There is more than enough for all of you.'

They feasted.

Down in the ravine, the jackals started howling again, awaiting their turn. The bones would be theirs. Only the cellphone would be rejected.